MW00680280

"Remaining true to his Uniontown roots, Dan writes a collection of down-to-earth vignettes of his simple beginnings in *Out of the Projects*. As his story unfolds, he relates life lessons reminding us that our experiences can be transformational. Sports, friendships, and ultimately, the love of his family, make Dan the wonderful human being he is today."

—Karen Fornari
Friend, educator and former colleague

A touching portrait of a determined young boy growing up in what some would consider adverse conditions, yet he used that adversity to his own benefit and succeeded."

Eaton Literary Agency

"*Out of the Projects* is a heartwarming story of childhood memories and lessons we all can relate to."

—Denise Lynch
Educator and friend

out of the PROJECTS

out of the PROJECTS

Overcoming Adversity Through Family and Sports

Charles Daniel Ross

TATE PUBLISHING & Enterprises

This book is designed to provide accurate and authoritative information with regard to the subject matter covered. This information is given with the understanding that neither the author nor Tate Publishing, LLC is engaged in rendering legal, professional advice. Since the details of your situation are fact dependent, you should additionally seek the services of a competent professional.

The opinions expressed by the author are not necessarily those of Tate Publishing, LLC.

Published by Tate Publishing & Enterprises, LLC
127 E. Trade Center Terrace | Mustang, Oklahoma 73064 USA
1.888.361.9473 | www.tatepublishing.com

Tate Publishing is committed to excellence in the publishing industry. The company reflects the philosophy established by the founders, based on Psalm 68:11,
"The Lord gave the word and great was the company of those who published it."

Book design copyright © 2009 by Tate Publishing, LLC. All rights reserved.
Cover design by Amber Lee
Interior design by Kellie Southerland

Published in the United States of America

ISBN: 978-1-60799-276-9
1. Biography & Autobiography, General
2. Sports & Recreation, General
09.04.06

"How does a teacher make a lifelong impact on a student? He quietly teaches those lessons that help a student best succeed in life, long past graduation.

I was fortunate enough to have such a teacher who believed in me far more than I believed in myself. We met in 1979—Mr. Ross was my sixth grade teacher.

When Dan Ross wasn't in the classroom, he was on the track, on the basketball court, or on the cross country course, as he coached teens for over thirty-five years. As a student-athlete, I spent my teen years participating on Mr. Ross' teams. I'm only one of many Dan Ross' kids who benefited from Dan's selfless gifts of time, devotion, and encouragement.

Looking back now I can appreciate the lessons this teacher and coach taught us as we sweated and struggled as a team. Lessons in sportsmanship, teamwork, respect for others, dedication, and determination were a powerful influence on a young teen. The "Mr. Ross Lessons" gave me the confidence, not just as a struggling athlete, but more importantly, the confidence to face life's obstacles, to stand up for my beliefs, to treat others with respect, and most of all, to believe in myself.

Of course, during those teen years, I did not tune-in to the whole "life lessons" concept. I just knew that there was something that kept me on task—I didn't want to let Mr. Ross down. During my adult years, I've been blessed with having Dan Ross in my life again. I've learned of Dan's years growing up in the projects of Uniontown, PA. I understand now how his early years provided the lessons he shared with today's youth and even an old kid like me.

On behalf of the many, many youth whose lives were enriched by Dan Ross, I extend my thanks to you, Mr. Ross, for reminding us that we still have lessons to learn—long past graduation. "

—Kristine Tedder

In the late 1970s, when I had graduated from college and moved away from home I started to have a very uneasy feeling about my old homestead, Lemon Wood Acres in Uniontown, Pennsylvania. My mom continued to reside in Lemon Wood after my brother Ted and I had moved on to pursue our individual careers, me as an elementary teacher in Pittsburgh, PA. and Ted as a social worker in Harrisburg, PA.

My brother and I started to become increasingly fearful about what was happening in the old neighborhood. Mom would often call Ted or me to complain about how the neighborhood had started to change. Break-ins were becoming commonplace. Drug trafficking and daily violence had become the norm. State police cruisers were constantly patrolling this now, high risk crime area.

One day while my mom was upstairs talking to me on the phone she heard someone breaking into the house. I pleaded with her to hang up the phone and call the police. She did so immediately! That was the final straw for my brother and me. We had to uproot our mother from her home of thirty-some years because it was no longer safe.

A decade or so later, Lemon Wood Acres had physically deteriorated and became such a haven for drugs, alcohol and prostitution that the county decided that it was in the public's best interest to demolish the development in the early 2000s.

There were many scathing articles written in the local newspaper about Lemon Wood and the families that dwelled there. I was deeply saddened when I read some of the accounts because I had a very different perspective.

The Lemon Wood Acres that I remembered was filled with loving, caring, hardworking families. Those kids that grow up in those special families, many came to be my good friends. We all shared a very special bond which was a true compassion for sports, not the drugs and alcohol so prevalent today! Through sports we were able to tackle many of the daily obstacles and pressures that life had to offer and in doing so we learned what was truly important in life.

Out of the Projects is dedicated to all the boys and girls who grew up with me and became strong men and women of today.

CONTENTS

Growing up in Lemon Wood Acres, a housing project in Uniontown, Pennsylvania, provided me with a lifetime of joyous memories. What made the projects, often referred to as the Jects, so special were the people—all different, yet all the same—who were searching for the American Dream of a better life and greater opportunity. This is my story, but it could be the story of almost anyone who shares the roots of my hometown—brothers, sisters, relatives, and friends. We shared a common heritage or bond. We lived in the projects.

MY FAMILY

My father and mother moved to Lemon Wood Acres in October 1950 just after my brother Ted was born. The housing authority had just completed the initial phase of the project construction. One year after my parents moved in, I was born.

Mom and Dad were caring and loving, but they were very different from each other. Dad, a man of few words, was quiet and private. When he spoke, he had his children's immediate attention.

Dad never had the opportunity to finish high school. Like many others during his era, he quit school after the ninth grade to help support his family. Despite his limited education, my father was the brightest person I ever knew. A self-taught man, he had a tremendous thirst for knowledge, learning advanced engineering and electronics.

That, however, isn't why I feel he was extraordinary. It was the way he looked at the world and the people around him. He had profound perception. Though he wanted nothing for himself, he always wanted our family to have a better life than his. He knew that education was the key to that change. He believed that anyone willing to work hard and sacrifice, if given the chance, could accomplish anything.

Dad never said much about his childhood, but, from what I could piece together, his parents died when he was young. He was raised by close relatives whom we called Uncle Jim and Aunt Isabella. They told me that Dad worked before and after school, often getting up at four o'clock in the morning to deliver newspapers, while after school he did odd jobs in the neighborhood. Uncle Jim said Dad worked twelve to fifteen hours a day as a teen.

Life for my father was difficult, as I can only imagine. Being an only child made him quiet and private about his youth. I was certain of one thing—he wanted a better life for his family.

Mom was vastly different from Dad in all respects. She was very outspoken. If she had something on her mind, she said it with conviction. Perhaps the reason for her being so loud was her early upbringing. Mom was raised in a family with seventeen brothers and sisters.

I couldn't imagine what mealtime was like in the Ford household. No wonder Grandpa and Grandma never smiled in any of their pictures. With eighteen kids, would anyone?

Mom had the benefit of a high-school education, as did many of her brothers and sisters. She, like Dad, understood the value of a good education and the benefits that would come from it. In the Ross household, education was the key to the door of opportunity.

Mom and Dad married in 1951. I was born that same year and was named Charles Daniel Ross. Charles was after my grandfather, while Daniel was after Mom's brother.

All I know about my early years came from Mom. She said she and Dad worried about me during those years because I had many health problems. Once I developed measles that went to my kidneys, and I had to be hospitalized and placed in isolation for a long time. The doctors didn't think I'd live long. Fortunately for me, I seemed to have a guardian angel to help me through troubled times.

My parents believed in change bringing a better future. The biggest change for us came when we moved to Lemon Wood Acres, a huge step. It was the closest we came to living in a house of our own—vastly different from our previous living situation.

At 145 Lemon Wood Acres, we had a two bedroom house with a living room, dining room, kitchenette, and a large, open, grass field beside the house where we kids could run and play. To some that might have been small, but for us it was like a palace. Most importantly, it became our home for several decades.

TIES THAT BIND

Growing up in the projects was bitter-sweet. It was bitter, because we were poor, though not dirt poor, just comfortable. We had food for every meal, clothes, and shoes but very little else.

Our experience was sweet because ties of close kinship existed between the rows of tenants at Lemon Wood Acres. Black and White families lived side by side, sharing space and time. Although we struggled daily, there was the encouragement of knowing we didn't struggle alone. We helped each other through times of despair. That enabled all to find the strength and courage to keep moving and continue working hard toward our goals. In the backs of our minds, we knew we had someone to lean on and call a friend.

THE NEIGHBORS

People made the projects a unique place to live. The Browns, who lived next door in #147, moved in approximately the same time as my parents. Mary and William Brown had two daughters, BB and Brenda. Later, Patty and Lydia were born, and then came Junior. After Junior, Mr. Brown said he had enough children.

Pat, my favorite in the Brown household, was my best friend during my adolescent years. We were both born in 1951, she in August, I in October. We grew up sharing a special bond of friendship and trust. We even shared childhood diseases, including chicken pox, measles, and the mumps.

Sometime after sixth or seventh grade, Pat and I grew apart. I became an athlete. She became a young lady. In a later decade, we probably wouldn't have drifted apart. She was a tremendous athlete, but during the sixties it wasn't fashionable for girls to participate in physical endeavors other than band, chorus, or cheerleading. That was a pity, because Pat would've been a champion.

Thoughts of the Browns always conjure special, vivid memories. Mrs. Brown was the world's best baker. That was my personal opinion, but I knew my family members shared it. We could smell the aroma of her baking a quarter mile away. The smell of those fresh-baked goods made our mouths water and stomachs churn.

Anytime she baked, usually once a week, she sent over a pan of piping hot fresh baked rolls that melted in my mouth. I was a picky eater as a kid, but her fresh baked rolls were wonderful. Even thinking about them makes me hungry.

On the other side of our house lived Ms. Gwynee and her grandson, Carlton Black, whom we called Chubby. As a preteen, he was five feet eleven inches tall and weighed over two hundred pounds. His heart almost matched his size. He would give someone anything he had if that person needed it.

One of my saddest memories from my days in Lemon Wood was when Ms. Gwynee and Chubby moved to Chicago to live with Chubby's mother. They didn't return to Uniontown often, but Mom corresponded with them frequently by phone and letter.

Much to our surprise, when Chubby graduated from high school and came to visit us, he wasn't chubby anymore! He was six-feet-eight-inches tall and 245 pounds of solid muscle, an All-Chicago football star and recent recipient of a major college football scholarship. Since the nickname Chubby didn't fit anymore, we called him Carlton.

Reverend and Mrs. Hickenbottom occupied the house beyond the Browns'. They had two daughters and three sons. I never felt a need to be close to the girls due to our age difference, but I liked Sylvester, the oldest of the teenage brothers. He was always friendly with the neighborhood kids and very upbeat and positive.

What I remember most about him was that he always sang, no matter what he did. He had a great singing voice. He, along with his entire family, sang in his father's church on Sundays. Often, during the week, Sylvester talked the young bucks—his term of endearment for the young kids in the neighborhood—into singing a song by the Temptations, the Four Tops, or a religious tune while standing on a street corner during warm summer evenings.

Sylvester's two younger brothers, Norman and James were very different. Norman was a bully, not someone very personable or friendly. James, a cross of his two brothers, was tolerable most of the time, but he always acted as though he were better than they.

Reverend and Mrs. Hickenbottom were very strict,

hardworking and religious people. They eventually moved to Virginia My cousins, the Fants, moved into their tenement.

best friends—
THE THREE STOOGES

I grew up with a host of talented and colorful characters. Of the group, my friend Larry and my brother, Ted, were my closest friends. The three of us were often called the Three Stooges. Ted was Moe because he was the oldest and enjoyed bossing Larry and me around. He was always serious. Everything had to be done his way.

Larry was part clown and instigator, always in the middle of things and ready to jump into an adventure on a moment's notice. Larry, nicknamed Speedy, was my best friend until I went to college in 1969.

Larry was raised by his grandparents, Mr. and Mrs. Wallace Thomas. The Thomas's moved to the Jects when I was in the fifth grade. Larry and I were instant friends. We became constant companions on the baseball diamond at school, on the basketball court, and on the playground. During that time, we developed a bond of true friendship, love, and trust that paved the way for many memorable experiences.

Larry wasn't a typical project kid. He didn't have holes in his jeans or patches on his pants. In the Jects a patch was a badge of honor for a member of the Acre Crew. He didn't wear the same shirt twice in one week, nor did he wear the same pair of pants. Furthermore, he always had money. Though he didn't fit the mold of a Crew member, I accepted him. Some of the others perceived Larry as being rich because of his grandparents' persona. They had a big beautiful car, a lot of nice household items, plenty to eat and money to do some of the extras that most of the families just couldn't afford.

Mr. Thomas, at times, could be a bit harsh and often voiced his displeasure to Larry about some of his new found "project" friends. Larry seemed to be embarrassed by having this undue attention thrust upon him being the new kid on the block. I give Larry credit though; he was always more then willing to share whatever he had with those around him. However, Larry's true sense of friendship was immeasurable in my book.

The third member of the Stooges, playing lovable Curly, was me. I was a carefree, happy-go-lucky clown, always poking fun, looking for something to liven up the day. On this day in particular we decided to try our hand at high jumping. We gathered some old discarded mattresses, pounded two small posts into the ground for standards and found a long piece of clothes line string to serve as the high jump bar.

Ted was being his normal bossy self trying to direct the show. I was attempting to place the mats in the proper area in order for us to have a safe jump. I would move the mat in one direction; Ted would pull it back to another spot. I would move it back; he would start to move it back. Then I would just dive on the mattress so he couldn't move it, then Larry would follow suit. Ted would get so mad and we loved it.

Finally we were all getting a little impatient. The standards weren't holding firm as we had anticipated. We needed to start jumping or this would be a huge waste of an afternoon.

Larry yelled, "I'm just going to jump. Get out the way!" Larry started his approach and rolled over the bar onto the mattress landing very awkwardly on his arm. Larry was lying there in obvious pain and Ted stated. "Get up Larry! There's nothing wrong with you." Larry said, "It's my arm!" Ted said, "Let me see it!"

Ted took Larry's arm and started to exam it by moving it back and forth, pulling and bending it while proclaiming, "It's alright! It's alright! Stop being such a baby!"

I knew there was something seriously wrong because

Larry did seem to be in a lot of pain. I told Ted, "I think we need to take Larry home."

Ted grudgingly agreed. We walked Larry slowly up to his house and Mrs. Thomas looked at his arm and thought it would be best to take him to the hospital. She called her husband and they drove Larry to the Uniontown Hospital. Sure enough, Larry was diagnosed with a broken arm. He would have to stay in the hospital overnight and have his arm set in the morning.

When Larry came home from the hospital Ted and I went over to see how he was doing and to sign his cast. We talked about our high jump adventure and hysterically laughed about Dr. Ted's examination.

"What a smooth move!"

So for now, we would just have to postpone our high jump contest for another time. So, is anyone up for a nice friendly game of Monopoly?.

That's how I passed the time with Larry, as his arm healed over the next several weeks, playing board games, watching TV, playing cards, listening to records and just acting silly. It was fun but it wouldn't replace the excitement of the outdoors. Everything that we did outside seemed to involve running games. Whether it was a classic game of release, touch football, hide and seek, 4 square, red light–green light, or cowboys and Indians, it didn't matter. They all involved running. Larry wasn't participating because he might fall and re-injure his arm so he would be the official starter or judge for what we were doing.

Time passed quickly and Larry had his cast removed and was given the doctor's okay to resume physical activity and everyone knew what that meant. It was time to take it to the blacktop, which was the real game of choice.

FOR HONOR AND GLORY

Once, when the Three Stooges and several other members of the Acre Crew were in our early teens, we decided to take the Crew down to our favorite play area, the Lincoln-View Playground, one of eight playgrounds in Uniontown. On that particular day, we decided to play basketball with a group of friends from the lower part of the Jects.

Often during this spirited rivalry between the upper and lower part of the Jects, controversy reared its ugly head in the quest for bragging rights on the blacktop.

One day Bill Slanders, a resident of Lemon Wood, was driving hard to the basket at the end of a game. Larry fouled him by pushing him from behind into the basket support. Bill fell to the pavement, dazed but not seriously injured.

Recovering from his fall, Bill stood slowly, his expression murderous. Since I was the closest player to him on the court, he thought I'd shoved him. A vehement argument ensued about whether I was the offender. I very loudly stated my innocence, but he didn't believe me. Tempers were short.

As tension escalated, one thing led to another. There was a push and then a shove; then the fight was on. I felt like David fighting Goliath. What happened next was a big surprise! Ted decided his little brother needed some help. Although I wouldn't have admitted it then, I probably did.

Ted jumped into the arena and stood between Bill and me, then challenged him. I felt upset. I couldn't let my big brother fight for me. I told him to butt out. "This is my fight, not yours."

Ted, feeling like my protector, decided I was wrong. He didn't want anyone hitting his little brother. "If there's any fighting to be done, I'm the one to do it."

I disagreed loudly, but Ted always got his way. I wondered why no one ever listened to me.

The end result of the conflict resulted in a Joe Frazier versus Muhammad Ali fight. Much to everyone's surprise, Ted and I began slugging it out! It wasn't that good a fight, more like hockey, with a lot of dancing around and very little contact.

Then Larry jumped in to restrain both of us, trying to create a peaceful settlement to the mess he created. While that went on, Bill with fist clenched and ready to fight, waited to take on the winner.

Unfortunately, with Larry involved, there was no clear-cut winner. What should we do? We couldn't let Bill walk away without finishing the battle. There was no honor in that.

Dad always said, "What you start, you must finish," though I doubted he meant fighting when he said that.

Since Larry started the whole thing, the Three Stooges arrived at a compromise. Moe, Larry, and I united against Bill. David against Goliath became a battle royal. Bill left the court a battered man, and the three of us left for home—friends.

my first love as a youth—
BASEBALL

Sports were an important part of my life and the lives of other members of the Crew, too. When I was eight or nine, baseball was my favorite sport. I played third base, often called the hot corner, and centerfield. I began my formal Little League at Bailey Park at age nine. My team was the Orioles and my first Little League coach was Mr. Fink.

When we started practice, Mr. Fink had only two weeks to prepare us. He had each of us try positions in the infield and outfield to see where we played best. I made the first team as third baseman because I was one of the few players who could throw straight enough for the first baseman to catch the ball without too much difficulty.

Mr. Fink seemed to have everything

well organized and under control before the first game. Unfortunately, he forgot one key component of the team—the pitcher. All during practice he or another parent pitched to us during batting practice. Who would be our pitcher?

Mr. Fink decided to let Elroy, his son, pitch. When the Braves were up, Elroy's pitches were hit almost every time, and the Braves scored several runs. Finally the inning ended.

Jeff Tarpley was on the opposing team, another member of the Crew. He was slated to pitch for the Braves that day. I never liked Jeff, because when he moved to the Jects, he tried to steal Patty, my childhood sweetheart.

Jeff went out to the mound. Every time I stepped up to bat, I pretended the ball was his head. That day, I had a single, double, triple, and home run. Despite such success, that wasn't why my first Little League game was so memorable.

Elroy struggled when he pitched. The next inning was the same, and we were behind by several runs. Finally, Coach Fink told me to try pitching, thinking if I was strong enough to throw the ball from third base to first, I should be able to throw to home, too. He was wrong.

In my pitching debut, I hit the first batter with a fast ball in the leg. The second batter received another fast ball in the arm, while the third batter tried to turn away from an inside pitch and was struck in the back. While all three runners stood on the bases, holding various parts of their anatomies, the next batter nervously stepped forward.

I wondered what he was thinking. I'd thrown only three pitches, and each had hit the target. That was a good average. Would he become victim number four?

I went into my windup and threw the ball toward home plate. The pitch was high, fast, and wild. The batter ducked to keep from being beaned on the head. What came next was a first in Little League History at Bailey Park. The umpire called time out and told Mr. Fink I was through pitching. I was sent back to third base and never pitched again in Little League. The umpire was afraid I'd hurt someone. I felt it was just a little control problem, something I could correct with a few dozen batters.

We lost the game ten to nine. I experienced the agony and ecstasy of sports all in one game. I can't help but think I could've been the next Bob Gibson or Satchel Page if only the umpire had let me pitch.

SIBLING RIVALRY

Ted and I were close in age, only 362 days apart. Big brother always acted much older than I. To minimize this natural rivalry, we unconsciously took opposite roles and positions. He played outfield, and I played infield. Ted was a distance runner, so I was a sprinter and jumper. He was talkative, while I was quiet.

Mom and Dad felt that keeping us tired would keep us out of trouble, so they encouraged us to play sports.

Baseball at Lemon Wood Acres was as fun and exciting as at Bailey Park. Usually our games were highly competitive and very emotional. Some games lasted a week. Most often the game was called when we lost the ball in the weeds or players were called home by family members or it became too dark to play.

Ted and I were called home fairly often. One incident helped fuel our sibling rivalry.

Dad was quiet but fair, a strict disciplinarian who didn't tolerate nonsense. We had a strict, regimented routine we followed. Breaking it meant suffering the consequences, which were often severe and painful.

One day we continued the battle for Upper/Lower Championship of the Jects. It was a warm and beautiful day. We started in the morning, took a break for lunch, and started again at 3:30PM.

After playing for an hour, I knew it was near dinnertime and Ted and I needed to go home. There were two outs, a batter at the plate, and Ted was pitching. I told him it was time to go. He said he'd be there in a few minutes, so I left without him.

That was my first mistake. I should've waited. Once I arrived home, I washed up and sat with Mom and Dad, waiting for Ted. Time passed slowly.

The reason for the delay was two-out lightning stuck. That meant there were two outs. Then the losing team began to rally, so Ted played for another twenty minutes. After the rally, Ted sprinted up the hill and ran into the house without word. He washed up and took his seat at the dinner table while Mom and Dad watched.

Dad was upset with Ted's tardiness and angry over big brother's lack of responsibility and respect. He quietly asked Ted to leave the table and go to bed without his supper.

As I sat there ready to eat, my stomach grumbling, my parents stared at me. "What did I do?" I asked.

"You should have waited for him. You know that one of our family rules is if you leave together, you come home together."

I, too, was sent away without my supper. I had to join Ted and wait for Dad. I ran up the steps as a wave of anger engulfed me. I considered the chain of events that occurred and became too upset. I was ready to fight the world. Since my world was the bedroom, I needed to be master of that domain.

When I walked in, Ted sat there, smiling. "Why didn't you come when I asked you to?" I asked. "You never listen to me when we do things together, and we always end up in trouble!" He sat and smiled. His attitude upset me so much I wanted to hit him. True to form, Ted wouldn't hear of it. We continued our verbal exchange, and then there was a push and then a shove. We were fighting. It was the only time I can recall having a fistfight with Ted. Of course, I was losing.

As we sparred and wrestled, I slammed a hard right cross at him. Ted ducked, and I hit the wall. Later, I learned I broke my hand.

The fight ended as abruptly as it began when we thought we heard footsteps. If Mom or Dad found us fighting, we'd be in even bigger trouble. I never let on

I was in pain. The code of the street was to never let anyone see you sweat. We declared the fight a draw. Ted probably won, but I'd never admit defeat.

The hardest part over the next few days was hiding my swollen hand from my parents. I managed so well not even Ted suspected.

About a week later, I was in Mr. Hooks' gym class. As we played basketball, someone threw me a hard pass, and the ball struck my injured hand. I grabbed it in pain. "Can I see that hand?" Mr. Hooks asked. He took me aside, examined my hand, and said I should have it checked by a doctor.

When I went home that day, I told Mom what Mr. Hooks said, and she took me on the bus to the Uniontown Hospital. They x-rayed my hand and said I crushed my knuckles. It would require surgery and two pins to correct the problem.

The final result of my sibling rivalry was that I missed my only chance to play basketball at the junior-high level. That was the bad news. The good news was Mom and Dad never knew how I broke my hand. If they did, they would've killed me.

Fighting was a "no-no" in the Ross household. My parents felt very strongly against acts of physical violence but they did believe that you have the right to defend yourself when your life is threatened. I didn't think the altercation that I had with my brother would

have applied to their general rule of thumb and I defi-
nitely wasn't going to test the waters so this was one
secret that I kept to myself.

FAMILY RULES

Mom and Dad had a simple parenting philosophy. One of their favorite principles was to keep us tired and out of trouble. My brother and I were always involved in something. In the fall, because my parents wouldn't let us play football, it was cross-country. In the winter it was basketball. In the spring it was track and field and baseball. Our summers were spent playing basketball, baseball, and participating in playground-sponsored activities.

Most of the Crew members included themselves in those activities too. The sport in which we excelled most was track and field.

As long as I could remember, I ran. Every game we invented to play as kids revolved around running. At night we played "Release, It Tag, and Pass Anywhere." As long as it involved running, everyone in the Jects played. We had a blast.

One of our favorite Friday-night activities was Lemon Wood Acre Downs. That was a race set up by the older Crew members who recruited the young ones to serve as their racehorses for the evening.

Those of us who were horses went to the top of the street and waited for the words, "Take your mark, set, and go!" The older Crew members bet on who'd win each race. I was often the winner. For doing such a great job, I was treated to a can of pop or some ice cream by my owner or benefactor. Looking back I see it was child exploitation, but we didn't mind. We loved to run no matter the reason.

THE PLAYGROUND

Most of my friends and I grew up at the Lincoln View Playground in Uniontown, where we spent almost all our summer days and nights. The playground had many games, including Ping Pong, volleyball, four square, table hockey, whiffle ball, shuffleboard, basketball, and tether ball. We had sleep-outs, cookouts, movies, and other special events, too. In the sixties in Uniontown, the playgrounds were a happening place.

Even with such a wide variety of games and activities, the favorite event for me and other Acre Crew members was the yearly intra-city track and field championship. In all the years of the playground association's track-and-field competition, East End Playground was the only site that won the coveted award.

The East End site boasted some of the finest athletes ever to don a uniform. Some of the names including Sandy Stephens, All-American at Minnesota; Stu Lanza, All-American at Nebraska and a former Laker; Ben Gregory, Nebraska University and Buffalo Bulls; Ray Parson, Minnesota and Detroit Lions; Nelson Munice, the Browns; and Chuckie Munice, California University and San Diego.

With such a list of outstanding athletes living in the East End, winning the track-and-field championship always seemed a foregone conclusion. The other playgrounds could fight over second place.

That may've been the case in the early sixties, but the Crew had arrived. Ruby Laskey, the Lincoln View playground director, was the coordinator for the track-and-field meet. When she had tryouts for specific events, we saw her smiling as the preliminaries began.

One by one a Crew member stepped up for his or her specialty. Time and again, we broke records, not by fractions of seconds or inches, but by entire seconds, inches, and feet. Whatever the event, the outcome was always the same, with a member of the Crew leading the way. Ruby knew she had something special, and history was about to be made.

THE MEET

The track meet was to be held on Friday at Bailey Park. Normally it took place at the Uniontown football stadium, but that was under construction. During the preceding week, Ruby was a nervous wreck, acting like it was the Olympic Games. Maybe it was a mini-Olympiad. It certainly was an elaborate production. Calling together the best athletes from the many different neighborhoods gave the event a special flavor no other summer activity could match. It was an awesome spectacle, but for us it had no particular meaning. It was just something we loved to do.

Friday, the day of the race, was like any other day. We went to the playground that morning. Ruby pleaded with us to make sure we would return on time. She must've reminded us of the starting time ninety-five times. We promised we'd be there on time, ready to go.

At the close of the morning playground session, we left for home. As we walked home, Lamont, my cousin, said, "Let's wear our gray sweatpants to the meet."

Most of us had those and agreed. While we were home, we ate briefly and gathered outside by the tree, our meeting place, dressed in gray sweats and looking like a real team.

There was Cedric Allen Tarpley, better known as Cat; Lamont Shannon, known as Lou or Scooby Do; Larry Thomas, known as LT or Speedy; Jake Ford; Hugh Fant, known as June Bug; Billy Brown, known as Junior; Bruce Fant; Montel Burke, known as Monty; Jeff Tarpley, known as JT; Ted Ross, known as Frog; and me.

The only Crew member not accounted for was Gerald McGifford, known as Skitchey. We couldn't leave without him, so we went to his house and knocked. Nancy, called Cookie, his sister, answered. She asked us to come in.

We found Skitchey sitting at the kitchen table, eating a twelve-cut Sicilian pizza, not dressed to run. We said it was time to go. He ignored us and kept eating. "What's the problem, Skitchey?" Lou asked.

"I don't have any gray sweats, so I'm not going." *Oh, boy!* I thought. What now?

Skitchey was an important member of our team. Without him, our success would be jeopardized. We discussed the dilemma among ourselves, but no one had any extra sweatpants. As we talked, Skitchey continued eating pizza. With two slices left, Monty realized he had an extra pair of sweats. He dashed home as Skitchey ate his eleventh slice.

As soon as Monty returned with the sweats, we were on our way to write the next chapter in sports history. Every step of the way, we prayed Skitchey wouldn't become sick.

Once we arrived at Bailey Park, Ruby sighed in relief. We kept our promise, and it was time for the games to begin.

As the meet progressed, the results were announced over the public-address system. "Long-jump winner, Dan Ross, Lincoln View; Fifty-yard dash winner, Gerald McGifford, Lincoln View; Seventy-five-yard dash winner, Lamont Shannon, Lincoln View; Softball-throw winner, Monty Burke, Lincoln View; Mile-run winner, Ted Ross, Lincoln View;" The list went on and on.

The Acre Crew made a dramatic impact on the score, and the balance of domination shifted from East End to Lincoln View.

We faced one last hurdle. It was the crowning jewel at the track-and-field meet—the four-by-one-hundred-meter shuttle relay, the last event of the day. It was said that was the race where legends were made and history was written.

The relay pitted the four fastest runners from each of the seven playgrounds to see who would win. The Lincoln View team consisted of Gerald "Skitchey," Larry "Speedy," Lamont "Lou," and me.

After waiting for what seemed like eternity for that event, all eyes were on us. The meet had already been won, but that race was what people wanted to see, because the winner would hold bragging rights as the city's fastest foursome.

The race began quickly. Gerald took a ten-yard lead and passed the baton to Larry, who moved out as if pushed from behind by invisible hands until he was leading by twenty yards. Larry passed the baton to Lou, who ran so fast he left the competition in the dust.

While that was going on, I stood beside some of the fastest guys in the city, all eager and anxious to receive their batons for the run down the home stretch. I always dreamed of such a moment, being in front of a huge crowd and running to the finish line, neck and neck with other young men, lunging for the tape at the last second to gain victory.

As Lamont approached, I saw something wasn't right. He was fifty yards ahead of the competition! *What about my dream*, I wondered, *and the race to the finish?*

He handed me the baton, and I stood there. In amazement, he shouted, "Run!"

I realized my dream wasn't coming true, so I jogged, not sprinted, my portion of the race. For an instant, I felt cheated of flashing to the finishing line, because the Acre Crew had done its job too well.

My personal moment wasn't realized, but it was still a banner day. We won Ruby her first and only track-and-field championship. The Acre Crew accomplished its goal, and I discovered the need for greater challenges.

HOOP DREAMS

Basketball ended up being my all-time favorite sport during my wonder years, but I didn't really enjoy it as a game until much later in life. I often played basketball, simply because I was told I couldn't.

I began playing hoops when I was in third grade at Phillips Elementary School in North Union Township, because Ted played as a fourth grader. I probably wouldn't have played if he hadn't. Sometimes little brothers emulate big brothers.

We often played one-on-one. Ted, not a bad basketball player, played on the team until ninth grade. During that time, he beat me constantly at one-on-one—until the summer of 1966.

We were playing our usual best-of-three series to fifteen. The rules were simple—no blood, no foul. That day's game was typical but with one slight change. I was winning.

I won the first game fifteen to thirteen, then the second fifteen to twelve. On the outside, I acted calmly about beating him for the first time, although my mind and heart were celebrating. I remembered the old adage, "Always act like you've been there." Ted showed emotion at the unexpected turn of events. He accused me of cheating, so we decided to play another set of three. I won each, with the margin getting bigger every game.

From then on, my perception of basketball changed for the better. Those beliefs that I couldn't play basketball were finally put to rest. I felt rejuvenated again!

Becoming more excited about practicing, I considered trying out for the ninth-grade team. The problem was the coach, Mr. Hoak. To play basketball, a person had to be big and tall. That philosophy caused me some concern. In the ninth grade, I was only five-feet-four-inches tall and weighed 105 pounds. When I was in seventh and eighth grades, I asked Mr. Hoak if I could try out, and he said, "You're too small, kid."

That year it would be different, or so I thought. Unfortunately, the fight with Ted gave me a broken hand one week before the tryouts, so I missed the ninth-grade season. I was very upset, but there was nothing I could do. That taught me an important lesson in life. We don't always get what we want, no matter how badly we want it.

During my convalescence, I was allowed to do only minimal activities with my right hand. Basketball and volleyball were out. Even with those restrictions, I remained relatively active.

I attended all home ninth-grade junior basketball games, though it wasn't easy. I saw my cousin Reed Mitchell on the team, and I wanted to be out there with him so badly. It wasn't fair.

One of the games that interested me was the North Union versus South Union contest. Buzzy Harrison, another cousin of mine, played for South Union, our cross-town rival. They had a great team that year, with Jim Hobgood, Red O'Brien, and Buzzy. I often found myself cheering for them, partly because I felt bitter toward Mr. Hoak for denying me the chance to play based on size.

During that basketball season, I kept busy with schoolwork, singing in chorus, and watching Ted and Larry play in the YMCA church league. After two months, it was time to have the pins removed from my hand, and I was allowed to resume normal activities within another week. By that time, the ninth-grade season was over, and I'd lost my chance to play for the junior high.

My dream of playing on the ninth-grade team never materialized, but something happened that had a profound effect on me for years to come. During the spring I had gym class with most of the boys on the ninth-grade team. The last gym-unit activity was basketball, and we played for three weeks straight.

I loved it. I played in every class as if I were in the NCAA finals. It was my chance to shine against the stars of the ninth-grade team.

After the final class of the year, as we walked downstairs, Mr. Hoak called me over. "Dan, why didn't you come out for the team?" he asked.

I wanted to say, "Because you said I was too small," but I didn't. Instead, I said, "I don't know." He smiled. "Well, you should have."

From that point on, I decided that I would never let someone's perception of me necessarily become my reality. If I worked hard, I knew I could achieve my goal.

a very SPECIAL SUMMER

During the summer of 1966, I continued my usual activities of baseball at Bailey Park, basketball at Lincoln View, and fun and games at the Jects. It seemed as if it would be a typical summer until Mr. Raho, my brother's English teacher and the administrator of a group that gave kids the chance to make money during the summer, contacted me and several other crew members to work in the tobacco fields. Ted went the previous year and had a good time, so we all signed on and spent the summer picking tobacco for AST, American Sumatra Tobacco, near Hartford, Connecticut. It was a great working experience.

We really learned the ins and outs of how tobacco was cultivated during those weeks. At camp we lived in a dormitory with approximately 250 boys for seven weeks. We were up at 7:30AM, ate breakfast, and worked from nine to five.

The work environment was spacious. We were driven or walked to gigantic tobacco fields of hundreds of acres that were roped off and covered with cheesecloth. Our job for the first couple of weeks was to straighten and sucker the plants. Suckering meant removing anything that attached itself to the root stem by tearing it off.

We scooted on our butts between rows of plants, straightening and suckering as we went. It wasn't a hard job, but it was very dirty. The juice from the plants collected on our hands and became extremely thick, turning black, and it was very difficult to remove.

Another problem was the high temperature working under the cheesecloth. It soared during the afternoons, making work very difficult. Then there were the snakes. They made suckering lower leaves dangerous, because they often hid under the large tobacco leaves to escape the heat. Fortunately for me, I never encountered a snake, but some of my friends did. I got the shakes every time I thought about it.

When working in the fields, we ate lunch out there. That wasn't easy with all the tobacco tar on our hands. We tried to wash it off and clean up before lunch, but it didn't work. Our hands were still filthy as we ate from our bag lunches, consisting of a piece of fruit, a peanut butter and jelly sandwich, a cookie, and something to drink.

The best part of the meal was the water brought in by water buffaloes. It was natural spring water, and it tasted better than soda. Most of the workers couldn't wait to reach the water buffalo. Some drank so much they became ill.

After several weeks of straightening and suckering plants, it was harvest time. We slid on our butts between the long rows, picking the lower leaves as we went. Once a group of eight to ten leaves was picked, I stacked them on the ground between the plants for a dragger to pick up. That was a person who came into the fields with a basket-like sled pulled by a long hook. He moved between the rows of plants and picked up the leaves we left behind.

Once the slide, or basket, was full, we took it to be loaded onto a truck, which took the baskets to a large barn, where the leaves were placed on a large, thin slat and hung to dry. Enormous heaters were set up under the leaves. When the barn was full of leaves, the heaters were turned on.

I didn't know how long it took to dry the leaves, but if people saw how tobacco was planted, cultivated, picked, chemically treated, and had to get that tar off their hands, they'd think twice before smoking or using any tobacco product. I easily imagined that tar collecting in someone's lungs as he smoked.

As the weeks passed, we became specialists, either draggers or pickers. Lamont, Marvin, and I were the best draggers in camp. Joe, the field boss, who was always red- eyed and sore about something because he drank too much, was stern and mean at times. He always shouted and cursed at us and was always in a foul mood, but I understood he had a job to do and a time-table to keep. In the tobacco business, time was money.

For some reason, though, Joe took a liking to us. Maybe he liked the way we worked. Though it was hard, we enjoyed it, and we managed to make it fun by turning it into a game. We called it "Beat the Picker."

The object of the game was to gain enough time to rest at the water buffalo. To do that, I, as a dragger, had to fill all the baskets with tobacco or leave none to fill, or I could catch up with the pickers and leave no tobacco to be picked up and dragged out. Either way, I was allowed to take a break.

I remember the first time we achieved our objective. All three of us sat around when Joe ran toward us, screaming loudly. When we told him we'd caught up with the pickers, and there was no tobacco on the ground. He checked and saw, to his amazement, it was true.

The next time he came to us to complain, all the baskets were full. That became the pattern. After a while, he became our friend, and he chuckled at the way we approached the job. By turning it into a game, we made a difficult task fun and enjoyable.

That summer's work experience led to the formation of the Brown Bombers, our cross-country dynasty. We left tobacco camp with rejuvenated spirits, money in our pockets for the fall, valuable work experience, and a new friend for life—Joe, the man we made smile!

coming of age— THE CROSS COUNTRY YEARS

The period between 1966 and 1969 was probably the best time of my life, as well as for many members of the Acre Crew. That was when most of us came of age. A major stepping stone for that transformation was cross-country season. There's no polite way to say it, but cross-country was a little boring at times. Running two to five miles over a cow pasture every day wasn't very glamorous, but that was what Ted, Lamont, Jeff, Marvin, Gerald, JB (Jerry Betters), and I did during football season. The only reason we stayed on the team was because we had fun together.

Mr. Peter Paul Kachur was our cross-country and track coach. He wasn't the most knowledgeable cross-country coach, but he was fun to be around. He had a good heart and strange sense of humor. One of the things I give him credit for was recognizing raw talent when he saw it and developing it to the best of his ability, given the poor facilities he had to work with during that time.

Mr. Kachur was great at delegating authority. He knew Ted possessed the most cross-country talent, so Ted was elected team varsity captain during my junior year, Ted's senior year. I ran on the junior varsity with Lamont, Marvin, and JB. Most of the time, Mr. Kachur briefly told Ted what to do, and we followed his lead, as did the other team members. During the season the varsity experienced many ups and downs as a team. The redeeming factor was always the JVs. Varsity might lose a close meet, but the JVs always won. That was the story of the entire season.

The junior varsity began making a name for itself throughout the county. We were known as the Brown Bombers—Lamont, Marvin, myself, and sometimes Jeff. Lamont always took the lead with Marvin, while I caught up at the half or quarter mile mark. Then all three of us ran shoulder-to-shoulder, stride for stride, for the rest of the race. It was an awesome sight that became commonplace as the season continued.

The varsity team, however, couldn't seem to get on track that season. One day before a race against Father Giebel High School, Mr. Kachur made it very clear in his pre-race speech that we needed to win that meet.

He also said that if we didn't perform to his satisfaction we'd have practice after the meet.

Ted, as usual, took first place for the Laurel Highland Mustangs, but he was followed by the Giebel runners. That wasn't a good sign. After all the runners were in and the score was tallied, varsity lost thirty-two to twenty-eight. The JV race followed, and we continued our domination; but that didn't seem to matter to Mr. Kachur.

After the JV race and after our opponents left, Mr. Kachur called a brief meeting at the starting line. Clearly unhappy with the team's performance, he said, "We're going to practice now."

Ted, who'd just won the first race, was having a bout of bronchitis, told Mr. Kachur, "I don't think I can run."

"Ross, if you can't run, go turn in your equipment," Mr. Kachur said, walking away. Ted walked away too.

Mr. Kachur came to the starting line, where the varsity and junior varsity teams waited, and saw Ted walking up over the hill. "Dan, where's your brother going?"

"I guess he's turning in his uniform," I replied.

Mr. Kachur's dream of having a winning season was walking away, but he was too proud to worry about it. He had a practice to run.

Cross-country without big brother was different, especially since Ted was the one who generally ran our practices. It seemed no one else wanted the job. Team morale sank lower each day. I knew Mr. Kachur sensed what was happening and knew something had to be done to keep the season from becoming a total disaster, but would he be willing to save face in the process?

Mr. Kachur chose to let the team decide if they wanted Ted to rejoin. Once put to a vote, Ted won twenty-three to one. I was the only one who voted against him. Our father said, "What you start, you have to finish, no matter what the circumstance. You don't quit."

Ted broke a family rule, so I voted against him. During the two weeks Ted was off the team, he'd done no running whatsoever but was still able to beat everyone on his first day back. That was truly amazing.

THE MERGER

In 1967 North Union and South Union high schools merged to form a new school district called Laurel Highlands. It was a strange match, but because of the economic situation most thought it was a good idea, because it would create a stronger tax base.

The only aspect that changed was we combined forces for all sporting events. The positive aspect for people like me who participated with the sporting team was meeting and interacting with different students. Through sports, I got to know many great student athletes from South. It was unfortunate that others didn't have the same opportunity.

That was the beginning of a very special time in my life, beginning with that fall's cross-country season. After that, it was basketball season.

For once, as basketball season approached, I was excited. Even though I never played on the junior-high team, I took advantage of other opportunities to play. I played in the Saturday recreational league that Mr. Harold "Horse" Taylor, the high-school coach, ran for elementary and junior-high players. I never missed a Saturday.

I worked and played hard in the recreational games to improve my skill level and knowledge of the game. I was surprised and relieved to make the junior varsity team my sophomore year, especially because we had two junior highs combining to make one junior-varsity team. I was also surprised to start on that team with my cousin Buzzy during the season. We had a tremendous year and great record.

The varsity team of 1966–67 was outstanding that season too. That was the first Laurel Highlands basketball team. The starting varsity consisted of Wil Robinson, Ray Yauger, Jeff Collier, Jon Kruper, and Jim Hobgood. They went undefeated at the exhibition and regular season, beating Uniontown twice during the year.

That was an amazing accomplishment, because Uniontown was a perennial powerhouse in Pennsylvania. The Laurel Highland Mustangs' only loss that season came at the hands of Mt. Lebanon High School in a triple overtime game in the WPIAL semifinals.

On the initial ride into the WPIAL, the Mustangs went twenty-seven to one and broke one of the longest winning streaks in the history of Pennsylvania basketball at that time by beating the Uniontown Red Raiders' home winning streak of eighty-plus games.

They raised the bar an extra measure for the next year's Mustang team.

RAISING THE BAR

The basketball season of 1967–68 for the Laurel Highland Mustangs will always be remembered as one of the most enjoyable times of my life. Only two starters from the previous year's twenty-seven-to-one team were back—Jim Hobgood and All-Stater Wil Robinson. Jimmy and Wilbert, though strong ball players, were very different individuals. Coming from different worlds, they weren't very good friends off the court. Once on the court, though, they played as teammates and worked in harmony to achieve the ultimate goal, winning the state crown.

That was my second year playing organized basketball for my school. During the summer we played in undergraduate tournaments at Laurel Highlands and Donora. I was surprised that Mr. Burke, the president of the Laurel Highlands Boosters Club, chose me as a starter during the summer. I knew I didn't have the offensive skill of many other players, because I'd never been taught those things, but I had great speed, was quick, and possessed tremendous heart. I also loved playing defense, at which I excelled, and that was the chief reason I became a starter.

With Jimmy and Wilbert, Buzzy Harrison, and Jim Rambo, we didn't need other individuals to shoot the ball. Accepting my role as defensive specialist, I loved it. Most of the time, I was amazed to be an integral part of the team equation for success.

My second year of playing organized basketball weighed heavily on me at times. I was often nervous and in awe of several of my teammates. There are always individuals who don't shine as stars but who still play significant roles. My personal favorite and key reason for our success, I feel, was Wayne Woods. Everyone called him Woody for short.

Woody was an all-conference football player who was big, strong, quick, agile, and temperamental. He was also the team clown. Even though he was unpredictable, when he decided to play, he was formidable. He was one of the first individuals who could be called the Enforcer. Woody was always in trouble with Mr. Taylor for something.

During the 1967–68 seasons, we played Mt. Pleasant at North Union High, the site of all Laurel Highland games. It was a typical contest between the two schools. We were always the dominant opponent for Mt. Pleasant.

On that night the score, with ten seconds to go, was 104–54, Laurel Highlands winning. Everyone on the team played that night except Woody. With approximately seven seconds left, Jim Rambo fouled out. Mr. Taylor looked down the bench and said, "Woods!"

Woody sat on the bench, still wearing his warm-up clothes, and ignored the call. "Woods, get in the game for Rambo!" Woody stood and slowly removed his warm-ups. "Woods hurry up and check in!" Mr. Taylor snapped.

Woody went to the scores table and checked into the game then walked to the opposing center and punched him before walking to the locker room.

The referee blew his whistle and gave Woody a technical foul for unsportsmanlike conduct. Woody was already gone. The Mt. Pleasant coach was outraged.

After the technical free throws, the final seconds of the game expired. Mr. Taylor sheepishly apologized to the Mt. Pleasant coach for Wayne's behavior. We knew what would soon happen in the locker room, because Mr. Taylor didn't allow such behavior from his players.

We followed Mr. Taylor as he rushed to the locker room to confront Woody. As he reached the room, he saw Woody walking toward the showers. Mr. Taylor walked up behind him, placed his hand on Woody's shoulder, and spun him around. I'd never seen the coach so angry before. "Woods, what did you hit him for?"

"Coach," Woody said calmly, "there wasn't time to do anything else." For the first time in his life, Mr. Taylor was speechless. What could he say in reply?

As the season continued, we faced our nemesis, the Uniontown Red Raiders. I had several cousins playing on that team, so it was always important when we played against them. In the first game, we beat them by one. In the rematch they beat us by one. Both teams having lost, the rules required a third game.

The section play-off was at the Pitt Fieldhouse in Pittsburgh, PA. Before traveling to the game, we had an early supper at the school cafeteria and boarded the bus for the trip.

Later that evening, fifteen busloads of screaming fans made the trip to support our efforts against the Raiders. The way the district responded was one of the great things about that time. Sports often brought our community closer together, even if it was for only a short time.

The game was for high stakes. The winner would continue in the WPIAL play-offs, and the loser would go home for good. The added pressure of being so close to continuing in the play-off or being eliminated took a toll on me. I played so poorly in the last Uniontown game, Mr. Taylor thought it best to start Tommy Bodgen in my place.

That was a good move. The game plan for the final rematch was to play a box-and-one on Bill Emmett, Uniontown's outstanding guard. Emmett had forty points in the last game, and we couldn't afford to let him do that again. Tommy would shadow Bill for several minutes. Then I traded with him.

We did our job that evening. Bill was held to only four points, and we beat the Red Raiders by twenty. We were the champs of section three, officially on our way to the play-offs.

In the first round of the play-offs, we defeated Jeannette High School. In the semifinals we beat Duquesne. Finally, we advanced to the WPIAL championship to play Donora, the media favorite to win that year. They had a talented group of players, including the Lomax brothers, Ken Griffey and Bernie Galiffa. Based on news reports, we were the fifteen-point underdogs. We, however, knew we could take them. We had beaten them in an earlier game during the summer undergraduate tournament.

Before the game we had our typical routine, a pregame meal in the cafeteria and a bus ride to the Burgh. That helped make us a little superstitious. We made sure we ate the same food, wore the same blazers, sat in the same seats to the game, and listened to the same songs. Nothing was allowed to change, or we felt we might lose. Fifteen busloads of students would follow a similar pattern later that evening.

The game would be a strong physical contest, and no one was prepared to back down. The contest started in typical fashion. Then disaster struck early in the first quarter. Tommy was making a sharp cut. Then suddenly he lay on the court, clutching his leg. He had fractured his ankle during his cut to the basket. I replaced him, and we continued our run. Because the game was getting so physical, Mr. Taylor decided we needed some extra muscle, so he sent Woody, the Enforcer, into the game. From that point on, the momentum began to shift in our favor. We never looked back again.

We won with a final score of seventy-four to fifty-three, but it was a bittersweet victory. Although we won the first WPIAL championship in our school's brief history, we lost Tommy for the remainder of the play-offs.

The next hurdle was the Western Regional Finals. We had to play the City League champs, Allegheny High. The winner would play in the state championship against the Eastern Regional winner. Allegheny was by far one of the most talented, athletic teams we played all season. They had outstandingly quick responses and great jumping ability.

In a packed Pitt Fieldhouse, we won a close decision, bringing us one step closer to the grand prize, the PIAA state crown.

The PIAA state championship, normally in the Harrisburg Farm Arena, was moved that year to the

Civic Arena in Pittsburgh for the first time in the tournament's history. We would play Cheltenham, led by All-State Captain Craig Littlepage.

We played before eleven thousand screaming fans, and it was a nail biter all the way. Neither team could establish a lead. Mr. Taylor used only six players during that game. Rich Wolinsky was the only sub called in.

The key moment of the battle was during the fourth quarter when Wilbert jumped high to block a shot by Littlepage. Had Littlepage gotten his shot, we probably would've lost. Because of that tremendous defensive effort, we forced the game into overtime—the first overtime in the tournament's history.

During the three-minute overtime, Jim Rambo became the man of the hour, netting several key baskets during that short time. With that, we managed to take control of the game, snatch victory from a previously undefeated team and clinch our first PIAA State Championship for the new Laurel Highlands School District.

It was a great feeling to see individuals from two historically rival school units brought closer together as communities, if only for a brief time. The effects of that championship stayed with my teammates and me a lifetime.

Although that basketball season was special, there were still more special moments to come in the months ahead. Spring signaled the beginning of track season. Ever since elementary school, I loved track and field.

My first track-and-field experience was at Phillips Elementary during the first elementary track-and-field championship held at North Union football stadium. We had a ragtag group of runners for participation in the meet.

The favorite was East Union and Fairground Elementary. During that day I won the seventy-five yard dash, the long jump, and ran one leg of the winning four-by-one hundred yard relay. We won the first track-and-field championship of North Union School District.

The following day, the newspaper came to the school and presented the trophy to Mr. Fodar, the principal, and I was elected the captain for scoring the most points for our team.

TRACK AND FIELD

After elementary school I continued running track in junior and senior high. Track was a lot different from basketball. Although it was considered a team sport, it was also an individual one. Mr. Kachur, our cross-country coach, was also the track coach. Ted was the track and field captain during the spring of 1968.

We never had much of a track tradition at either of the two merging schools that formed Laurel Highlands so there weren't many track and field awards in our school history. We always had a few good participants to make the season noteworthy. The key participants were Ted Ross, distance runner; Tom and Terry Ryan, middle-distance runners; Chase Holly, sprinter; Bobby Davis, triple jumper and sprinter; Bill Deshields, sprinter; and me, a sprinter and long jumper. Other participants included Lamont Shannon, Jeff Tarpley, Marvin Harris, Bob Yartz, Buzzy Harrison, Gary Harrison, Ed Regula, and Don Roddy.

We had a tough season in the spring of 1968. Ted, injured during the second meet that season, was unable to participate for the remainder of the year. I had a great year as a 220-yard sprinter, a member of the 880-yard sprint relay team, and as a long jumper. During the season, I set a school record for scoring the most points in Laurel Highlands' track and field history.

We ended the season with a record of three wins, five losses. Once track and field ended, the sporting season for the school year was over. All that was left was the annual all-sports banquet to honor the achievement of all the fine athletes and coaches. That banquet would be special for me because of the success of the basketball team winning the WPIAL and PIAA crowns.

At the banquet, various coaches went to the podium and made presentations honoring recipients one by one. In basketball Mr. Taylor presented the deserving Wil Robinson as the MVP for the season. I received an award for best defensive player that season, which made me feel really good. Few people in those days appreciated the defensive aspect of basketball.

When Mr. Kachur made his presentation, I received the biggest shock of my life. As he made his opening remarks, I felt anxiety and pressure building, but when he finally made his announcement I was stunned. "The award for most valuable track and field goes to Ted Ross!" He must've made a mistake, I thought. No, he means it! That was the only award I felt was truly mine. I set a school record for the most points scored in one season, and I broke the long-standing broad-jump record.

After the award presentation, Mr. Kachur came to me and explained his reasoning, but I didn't want to hear it.

"Dan, Ted was the heart and soul of our track and field program for several years, and we owed him a lot. It was unfortunate he was hurt, but I felt strongly that he should have the award. You're only a junior, and you'll have an opportunity to win the award next year." The only words I remembered were next year. What about the current year?

On our walk home from the banquet, Ted, with his two MVP awards for cross-country and track, and I, with my outstanding defensive award and team basketball award, talked endlessly about what I saw as an injustice—though Ted saw it as justice—concerning the presentation. Ted felt he deserved the award for his overall contribution. I disagreed very vociferously.

When we arrived home, our father greeted us and was elated to see his sons brought home trophies from the banquet. He never sided with either of us concerning the award. To him, we won it together. It didn't matter whose name was on the plate.

I disagreed. It mattered to me. I took a piece of tape that evening and wrote Dan Ross—Track and Field MVP 1968.

Nineteen Sixty Eight was a great school year in so many ways! A life lesson I learned was that through hard work, dedication and desire, dreams can come true. This year signaled my coming of age as an athlete. What a thrilling ride it was and it was just the beginning of more joyous times ahead.

TIME TO PREPARE

In the late spring and summer of 1968, I was still reeling from the success of our basketball program and the positive reaction that came from the community. It was a very special time, even with the loss of Wil Robinson, Jim Rambo, Wayne Woods, Rich Wolinsky and Bill Martin due to graduation; and Harry Jose and Pete Tracey to eligibility regulations; we still had a significant nucleus for the coming year.

That spring we hosted our own undergraduate tournament at the high school. Local teams from Uniontown, Connellsville, and Father Giebel came. The Mustangs, fresh off a state championship, were ready to take on all comers. We reached the championship in our tournament but finally lost in a close contest against Uniontown.

Doing better in the next season wouldn't be easy for the Mustangs. It was important to be ready to play hard.

THERE'S A SEASON
for every time

The summer of 1968 was the time when my big brother was preparing to leave for college. That was strange for me. Ted didn't follow the usual summer routine that the Acre Crew had. He was serious about everything and declined to participate in our normal summer activities.

In the fall he left for Penn State University. Originally, he'd been accepted at the Naval Academy in Annapolis, Maryland, but he failed the eye test. I felt our father wanted him to go to the Naval Academy, because he once served in the navy as a steward when Blacks were very restricted in what they could do and what rank they could hold. It was important for Dad to have a son attend the Academy and graduate as an officer.

Everything happens for a reason, and

Mom and Dad were still proud of Ted. So was I in my own way, but it meant something more to me than the others imagined. I'd finally have a room to myself.

I spent the last seventeen years sharing a room with someone, and it was natural for me to be elated because now I had a room to myself. I didn't have to worry about Ted getting mad at me or putting a tape line down the middle of the room to designate his side and my side. I didn't have to fear falling asleep first and having one of my Dad's wool navy blankets placed on me and waking up with hives all over my body the next morning. I no longer had to take that running start in the hallway in order to jump over the line that was placed in the doorway because Ted had laid claim to the entrance to our room.

I could celebrate now, for my room became my castle. I was the master of my domain. The only downside was I had to keep my domain clean. During chore time was when I realized how much I missed Ted's presence in the room.

As time passed I also realized that the positive aspect of sharing a room was that I learned how to become a very good long jumper due to all the additional practice that I to endure at the hand of my big brother.

GETTYSBURG

Another event that occurred during the summer of '68 was when Mr. Taylor, my high school coach, sent me to basketball camp in Gettysburg, Pennsylvania. That was my first trip to basketball camp, and I was excited. It was also my first trip away from home alone.

The day I was to leave, Mr. Taylor asked Dennis, his older son, to drive me to the bus. Something went wrong, and we missed the bus in Uniontown. The dispatcher said we could catch it at a stop thirty miles away, but we had only twenty-five minutes to make the trip.

We drove off at top speed. I worried about missing the connection, but Dennis got me there in time; and then I was off.

I arrived at camp late Sunday, sometime after six o'clock. All the other three-hundred-plus campers were dressed and sitting on the outside courts, listening to a lecture. I hurried to the dorm, checked in, ran to my room, dressed, and ran to the court. When I arrived, the speaker was completing his talk.

Most of the lecture was about the camp's rules and regulations and the behavior they expected from us in the dorm. It was strange being somewhere when I didn't know a soul. To my surprise, I made friends quickly and forgot about home.

During the first practice session that evening, we were doing competitive half-court drills, which were a lot of fun. While participating in some intense drills, I broke my only pair of glasses and had to do without them for the entire week.

Many talented ball players were there for the second week in the junior and senior divisions. I was in the senior division. Each player at camp was put on a team for a week. I played three games during the day. Between games, there were special drills that were held three times a day for an hour each.

Various coaches drilled us, or we had team practice. I wanted to say I played on the best team in camp, but that wasn't true. My team didn't win a game during the entire camp. Making it to the championship wasn't a possibility.

Even though our team didn't reach the play-offs, there were other enjoyable, stimulating activities. One of the special events was to have a select game each evening. Counselors and high school coaches selected the best players for the day, and those were divided into teams. Then the players competed on center court while the other campers watched. I was fortunate that week to earn a chance to play in all the select games, and I played well.

Another facet of camp was that I truly enjoyed the skill drills, which were designed to be competitive and required speed, stamina, and quick reaction time. I set several records while competing. The coach from Middletown, which won the Class B Boy's Championship, was always after me, because we won the Class A boy's title that year. There's always a little honest rivalry about who's the best in someone's state. I assumed that was why the Middletown coach tried to see if I could take it. To his amazement, I passed easily.

THE MOUNTAINEER

The guys at camp were great. They came from Pennsylvania, Maryland, New Jersey, New York, and West Virginia. One of the most memorable people was a fellow from West Virginia. I can't remember his name or what type of ballplayer he was, but I sure remember his peculiar eating habits.

He would eat anything for a price. The first night at camp, he made his offer known, and we tested him each night. Usually that involved fifteen to twenty campers paying money to see him eat something. His first challenge was when we offered him a large cockroach. There were stipulations on how something could be eaten. If he didn't follow the rules, all the money would be refunded to the spectators.

For the cockroach he couldn't just swallow it. He had to place it in his mouth, let it crawl around, begin chewing, then swallow. After following our instructions, he earned five dollars—easy money for someone who had a strong stomach.

The next night he said he'd eat a spider for eight dollars. We agreed and ran off to find a suitable spider. The search produced the biggest spider we could find, a wood spider. That thing was hairy and enormous! We gave the mountaineer the same instructions as the previous evening. Sure enough, he did as we asked. I couldn't believe it. The whole thing made me sick.

On the last night of camp, the mountaineer agreed to eat a frog for fifteen dollars. We pooled our money, and the search team, jar in hand, went outside to find the next victim while the rest of us waited anxiously.

They brought back a large jar with a three-inch toad inside. They passed the jar to the mountaineer, and he swallowed the innocent creature.

The spectators shouted for a refund. The crowd became ugly, because he hadn't followed the guidelines like before. They wanted their money back.

The mountaineer stuck his finger in the back of his throat and threw up the toad, which was covered with white mucus from being in his stomach. Then he picked it up, placed it in his mouth, and chewed before swallowing.

All I could say was that he was one guy who would never go hungry.

MVP

On the last day of camp, each division played championship games. Since my team hadn't won a game, we wouldn't be playing, so I dressed in my street clothes like many of the other campers, because right after the game, we'd have the closing ceremonies and leave for home. Someone would drive me to the bus station so I could catch the bus for Uniontown.

As I watched the senior division championship, I wished I were playing. There was a very good player on the white squad who'd been at camp for the past two weeks. In the dorm he often said he should've been MVP the previous week, and he was certain that if his team won the championship he'd be the Gettysburg Basketball Senior Division MVP.

I was sure of his claim. He had a strong week at camp, and he did a good job during drill and station work, but only the coaches could tell for sure. His team won the championship very convincingly. After the game all players were asked to sit in the stands. Mr. Carpenter began to announce the winner of the junior division league and all-tournament team for the week. Next was the senior division. He announced the senior division league champs one by one. Then he announced the all-star team, for which I was selected. Then came the moment of truth, it was time to announce the Senior Division MVP.

"The winner of this year's Senior Division MVP award is Dan Ross!" he said. That was one of the biggest surprises of my basketball life. I sat in the stands, watching the championship game because my team hadn't won a game all week, and wondered *how can this be?*

Many coaches and counselors felt I won the award with my work ethic in the station drills and the select games each evening. Another life lesson I learned at that camp was that it was important to stay focused and give it my all at all times. I never knew who might be watching.

Back home people were gearing up for fall. Conditioning for football season would start in a few weeks, and so did cross-country. When I arrived home from camp, I was excited about how well everything went. I met some great people and had some awesome experiences. Mr. Taylor was happy to hear of my success. Mr. Carpenter, the Rider College basketball coach, called and said he'd be checking on me during the season, adding that he liked what he'd seen at camp.

My first day back, I went to the courts like a man possessed. I played up a storm. Dennis, Mr. Taylor's oldest son, was impressed by my offensive transformation. I was always a good defensive player, but my offense was weak. Mr. Taylor knew it, which was why he sent me to camp.

One of the things I admired about him was his genuine concern about his players that went beyond his capacity as coach. He cared for us as individuals too. He always made us feel important, and he was willing to listen. There was no better feeling than knowing someone was on my side.

After returning from camp, I thought long and hard about doing cross-country. In my heart, when I heard that Lamont and Marv weren't running that season, I decided to concentrate on basketball instead. When Mr. Kachur learned that the Brown Bombers weren't running, he was very upset.

I felt bad about it, but my heart and soul weren't into it. It seemed that the real reason I ran was because of Ted and the other Crew members. We made it fun together. It wouldn't be the same without them.

Mr. Kachur was upset enough to drive up to Lemon Wood Acres to see us and hoped to change our minds. It didn't work. The Brown Bombers wouldn't be part of the cross-country equation that season. He became so infuriated that when school began he refused to speak to us when he saw us in the hall. Eventually that passed.

That was the beginning of my senior year in high school. I'd just made a difficult decision, and I was ready to make some academic changes to mark the next crossroads in my life. I hadn't thought seriously about the possibility of attending college because Ted was at Penn State and Dad had suffered a stroke that left him partially paralyzed. He couldn't work anymore, and his worker's compensation payment was low. Money was tight.

Furthermore, looking back on the situation, I realized that many of my teachers had very low expectations for many students of color. They often pushed Blacks into commercial or industrial tracks, like accounting, bookkeeping, typing, shop, metal work or woodwork. The rigorous track of foreign languages, advanced English, and mathematics were out of the question for most Black students.

Ted was an exceptional student, extremely bright and articulate. He was also a rebel and defiant at times, whereas most of the time I was on the coast cycle. I would've stayed that way if Mr. Taylor hadn't told me to improve if I wanted to play ball. After that conversation, I worked harder.

Even though I'd taken few academic courses, my grades were still pretty low. Finally, when Mr. Taylor talked with me about the possibility of a scholarship, did I realize my situation. He helped me see things in a different light, especially by saying that financial aid was available and many institutions offered full or partial scholarships.

Before any of that could become reality, I had some work to do to catch up academically. That meant making sacrifices, changing my work and study habits, and adjusting my priorities. Academics had to become number one.

My senior year of high school began with being selected to the Senior High Patrol at North Union. This was quite a surprise for me! Ted was a Senior Patrol member during the previous year. The Senior Patrol was a group of students who were chosen by the principal to be hall monitors. The patrols were to be positioned in the halls to make sure students walked on the correct side and to prevent vandalism or fighting. Those of us in the Patrol named ourselves the Triple-S PB, or Super Soul Senior Patrol Boys.

Being selected for the Patrol was an honor. In addition to hall duties, we were responsible for making announcements, delivering messages, taking students to the office, and, my favorite, setting up for the afternoon sock hops. I liked that last one, because we were paid each time we had to set up the music equipment, pull out the bleachers, and collect money.

It wasn't a difficult job. What was nice about it was it gave me the opportunity to have pocket money during the week. I didn't like to ask Mom or Dad if they had any spare change. I knew they were having a very difficult financial time because of Dad's poor health and his inability to work after he suffered a stroke in 1967. Money was in very short supply plus my parents had the added burden of trying to help my brother with his college expenses. With all that on their plate I felt very fortunate to have an opportunity to earn a few extra dollars during the week so that I could enjoy some of the things teenagers did such as: eat lunch in the cafeteria instead of packing one daily, attend a sock hop, travel to Winky's Restaurant for a Big Wink Hamburger after a Friday night basketball game or possibly take in a movie on a Saturday. It wasn't much but I didn't need much to make me happy.

For some reason, I was always finding ways to make a few extra dollars, not only for me but to help Mom and Dad. I would run errands for neighbors, cut grass or collect pop bottles to earn a few extra dollars. In the winter time I would often take a shovel and help people dig their car out of the snow or shovel someone's sidewalk or driveway. It wasn't a lot of money but every little bit helped in the long run.

I thought things were going okay but I knew Mom and Dad were still having a rough go of it. One day my Dad starting talking to me about what was to come next in my life. I had thought about college but put it in the very back of my mind. I knew how hard it was for them to have one son in college and I didn't want them to worry about dealing with the added burden of another. Dad told me his wishes for me and college. I took it all in but I really wasn't sure about it until my teacher and high school coach, Mr. Taylor spoke to me on the topic.

MORE HOOP DREAMS

I looked forward to another promising basketball season, but fate intervened once again. We had four of the top six players returning from our WPIAL and PIAA championship team. We also had a good JV basketball team that season. We lost a first team parade all-American in Wilbert Robinson. We wouldn't be able to replace him, but we felt we had enough talented players to take up the slack.

Before we began the season, several problems had to be overcome. Tommy Bodgen broke his ankle in the previous year's WPIAL championship, and we didn't know if he was fully recovered. My cousin, Buzzy Harrison, was injured as a member of the Mustangs' football team and underwent knee surgery, making him unavailable for the first part of the season. Jimmy Hobgood was being heavily recruited by several ACC schools, which was great, but two things happened to him that impacted our season.

First, he signed a letter of intent to attend the University of Virginia on a full basketball scholarship, which was wonderful. An outstanding shooter, he was a very knowledgeable player. He worked very hard over the years, and he deserved such an honor. The negative part of selecting a school early was that it sometimes changed a person's drive or focus. That seemed to happen to Jim that season.

During exhibition play we showed good promise as the season unfolded. We knew that once Buzzy was healed we could play well against anyone. That season we were fortunate to be asked to participate in the Johnstown War Memorial Tournament, one of the best high-school tournaments at the time. It had a list of some of the most outstanding ball players in the nation. Wilt Chamberlain was a former participant and MVP in that prestigious tournament.

The 1968 tournament included Johnstown, Mansfield, Meadville of New Jersey, and Laurel Highlands. The marquee players were Tom McMillan of Mansfield, Tony Venne of Johnstown, Alan Shaw of Meadville, and Jim Hobgood of Laurel Highlands.

The opening game pitted Mansfield against Meadville. It was billed as the Battle of the Giants, because it was rare to see two seven-footers playing on the court simultaneously. In the 1960s that was unheard of. We watched intently before going to the locker room to prepare for the host team.

Meadville just nipped Mansfield in the opener. The winner would play the nightcap the following evening, while the loser played the early game. The first half of each bracket was complete. To finalize it, however, we had to play Johnstown.

I had the honor of watching Johnstown's Tony Venne, an all-state candidate. We were able to defeat the hometown favorites that night despite playing before a hostile crowd. The next night, we would play Meadville in the championship.

From watching the opening game, we knew that Meadville's Alan Shaw would give us an enormous problem with his height advantage. Our tallest player was Jimmy Hobgood, six-feet-four-inches tall, while Shaw towered over us at seven feet. Mr. Taylor decided that I, standing at five feet ten inches, would watch Shaw.

What was I going to do? My job was to front him at all times with someone helping me on the weak side. The strategy almost worked, but he was a little too big and strong for me. We lost the game by a close decision, but that wasn't the reason it was so memorable.

After the game the tournament MVP was announced. There was a lot of hype about Jim Hobgood at the outset. The media wrote him up and spoke very favorably about him. He had two solid games in the tournament too. In the first game he scored nineteen points and seven rebounds, while in the second one he scored twenty points and eight rebounds. Those were great, but I felt that Buzzy, not Jim, should've been awarded the MVP.

Buzzy had seventeen points and fifteen rebounds in game one, with twenty points and sixteen rebounds in the championship, plus several steals. Sometimes I felt situations or outcomes were determined in advance before the facts were counted. That often cheated the special moments in other people's lives when they rose to the occasion and played supremely well.

I had a good tournament experience. Mr. Taylor later told me that Mr. Carpenter, a coach at Rider College who watched the games that evening, said once again that he liked how I played. He also promised to watch me closely as the season progressed.

The holiday tournament signaled the end of the exhibition season and beginning of section play. Uniontown, Connellsville, and Laurel Highlands were chosen as the top teams of our section, but the section was balanced from top to bottom. That meant we faced a dogfight for the league crown.

As the season progressed, Uniontown and Laurel Highlands were once again at the top of the standings. In our first encounter with the Red Raiders at

Uniontown, we were up by seven points going into the half, only to lose the lead and fall by twelve. That meant we were in second place.

The second half of the season played out in much the same way as the first. Both Uniontown and Laurel Highlands defeated all other section opponents. The rematch between our teams would be the last regular season game of the year, played at Laurel Highlands. If we won, we'd be tied for first place and would need a play-off game. If we lost, our season was over. Only the winner of each section would advance to the WPIAL play-off.

The final game was played before a packed house. It seemed that every home game we played for three years was sold out. Even some former players, like Wayne Woods, Ted Martin, and Wil Robinson, came.

This wasn't just a game. This was for city bragging rights for the year. This was the game that pitted cousin against cousin and friend against friend. This game was generally sold out weeks in advance. They always posted notices in the local newspaper and on the radio stations told people to, "Stay home if you didn't have a ticket because none would be sold at the door this evening!"

The game started in the usual fashion, both teams not wanting to give an inch. It was an extremely hard, clean fought, physical game that saw the lead see-sawed back and forth for three intense quarters. Then,

Uniontown slowly started to creep away in the fourth period.

That evening, I probably played the best defensive game of my life. There was one spectacular play that vividly comes to mind. My cousin, Arnie Belt, was the outstanding junior guard for Uniontown that season. His counterpart Basil Dickerson was equally formidable. On this one play the Red Raiders deflected a Mustang pass and it ended up in the hands of Belt. He, in turn, passed the ball to Dickerson to begin the infamous Raider fast break.

The two of them continued to quickly advance the ball down the court—passing, back and forth and back and forth. I was the only defender between them and an easy score to the basket, which would surely seal our fate that evening. I made a quick hedge fake to the ball and retreated backward into the lane and at that instant I was able to tip the ball away from the outstretched hands of Belt going in for a lay-up. It was truly an amazing play that excited the standing room only crowd but it wasn't enough that night. Our effort as a team fell short. We lost our bid for our third straight section crown by four points.

The next day in school, I was a little down and dejected after our loss to our arch cross-town rivals when Mr. Stephen Furin, the assistant principal and former basketball coach at North Union, came over to me to congratulate me on the outstanding defensive game that I had played last evening. He told me that I had batted away enough balls in that game to give us an opportunity to win and that's all you can ask for, any opportunity.

That was the end of not just our basketball season but it signaled the last time that I would have to share the court with Jimmy, Buzzy, Tommy and Reed Mitchell. We were upset, but all in all we had many wonderful, special memories from those glorious high school basketball days to last the rest of our lives.

DECISIONS

No sooner had basketball season ended then track and field began. Mr. Kachur stopped me in the hall one day and asked if I planned to run that season. That was the first time he spoke to me since I decided not to run cross-country.

My response came as a relief to him. I had two options for spring activities. I was selected to play in the Fayette County All-Star game, a unique honor. I put so much time and effort into basketball—that was a great reward for my years of hard work and sacrifice. However, during that time period, people who participated in an all-star game weren't eligible for any high-school spring sports, so track and field was out. I enjoyed running track, so my decision wasn't difficult. Mr. Taylor was probably disappointed that I didn't take the opportunity to play, but he understood. He knew, as did Mr. Kachur, that I loved to run. Chase Holly, Bob Davis, Bill Deshields, Tom and Terry Ryland, Ed Regula, Don Roddy, Buzzy and Gary Harrison, Tim Lulich, and I made up the nucleus for that year's team. We didn't have the number of athletes like many other teams we participated against, but we had a few strong points.

Tom and Terry Ryland and Tim Lulich were always good in the distance and middle-distance events. Chase, Bobby, Bill, and I were at our best in the various sprinting events. Bobby and I formed the jumping core. Bobby competed in high jump and triple jump, while I took the long jump. Team success was minimal, but individual performances were noteworthy.

The one event that became our team pride and joy was the 880-yard relay. During the season, we were undefeated in dual meet competition in that relay. That made Mr. Kachur proud. He was happy to finally have a winner.

At the conclusion of each season, the all-county track and field championship was held in Connellsville. The meet would involve all the schools in Fayette County. Once again, Connellsville was the favorite. They had a tremendous tradition of outstanding track and field activities, and the fact that they hosted the event added to their desire to compete at an even higher level, continuing their domination of the sport. We knew we faced a slim chance for a team award, but the 880-yard relay was our one glimmer of hope.

THE 880-YARD RELAY

The winner of the 880-yard relay would receive the A. J. Everhart trophy. A. J. Everhart, a high school English teacher, was one of the most successful coaches in track and basketball in the State of Pennsylvania. He did a lot to promote both sports during his tenure at Uniontown High. In his honor a special trophy was awarded to the winner of the 880-yard relay in the all-county meet. In past seasons, we never dreamed of winning that prestigious trophy, but in the spring of 1969, the relay team of Chase Holly, Bobby Davis, Dan Ross, and Bill Deshields was the team to beat.

The day of the meet, during school, Mr. Kachur called the members of the relay team together for a brief meeting before the trophy case. He already had a space cleared in it. He said that after we won the 880-yard relay, he'd have all our names engraved on it, then would place the trophy on display in the case forever. Excited about the possibility of being enshrined forever in the Laurel Highlands honors gallery, we felt confident we could do it. We had already defeated all competitors who would run that day at various dual meets during the season. That gave us a false sense of security.

The county meet would be held at the Connellsville High School track-and-field stadium starting at five o'clock. Preliminary events would run first, followed by the finals at seven o'clock. I was slated to participate in the long jump, 220-yard dash, and 880-yard relay.

My first event was the long jump. My stiffest competition would come from the Connellsville Falcons and Uniontown Red Raiders competitors.

The jumping event was very close throughout. A matter of inches separated the three of us. I was ahead for a while, but on the Falcon's last attempt, their jumper managed to jump a few more inches and won the long-jump title for that day. I finished in second place.

Next, I had to run the preliminaries of the 220-yard dash. There were several heats, and I needed to place in the top two to advance to the finals. I finished first in my heat and advanced to the finals, but they would be a lot tougher.

The top three runners were Francis Stroders of Connellsville, Jerry Wardell of Uniontown, and me.

I'd never beaten either of them during my high school sprinting days. They were top-flight runners with exceptional speed. Stroders had already placed first in the hundred-yard dash, edging out Wardell at the finish line. I knew that Jerry was out to avenge his defeat.

Although I felt nervous about the race, I tried to stay calm and run as relaxed a race as possible. Then the eight finalists were called to the starting line. Stroders, since he had the fastest time, was seeded first. Wardell, the second fastest, was seeded in the lane to Francis' right. I was seeded to his left. If the seeding process was done correctly, we would end in a "V" formation at the finish line.

Before the starting instructions, we exchanged pleasantries and wished each other well.

"Runners, stand at your blocks!" the starter called. "Runners, take your mark. Get set ... " *Bang!*

Francis shot from the block as if propelled by a missile. Wardell and I were close behind. At the 150 yard mark, it seemed as if Stroders had found a higher gear and began to pull away. Wardell was also inching out of my stride. At the finish line, it was Stroders, Wardell, and me.

Stroders ran a fantastic time that day of 21.9 seconds. Wardell's time was 22.4 seconds, followed by my 22.7. Even though I didn't win the 220-yard dash, I recorded my fastest time for the year and just missed the school record.

Many other Laurel Highlands athletes were doing well. Chase, Billy, Bobby and the Ryland brothers won medals, but as a team we weren't a contender for any honors. The only trophy we had a chance to win was the A. J. Everhart Memorial trophy. It seemed that was ours for the taking.

Before the 880-yard relay was called, we were done with our individual events. We sat around during the break, and I suggested we start passing the baton around, because it was almost time for the relay.

"We don't need to pass the baton around," Chase said. "This race is in the bag."

My teammates echoed his sentiment at the thought of warming up for the relay. In their minds we had already defeated each of our opponents, and there was no way they could challenge us in that event. Even with Connellsville's Stroders, the hundred- and two-hundred-yard champion, or Uniontown's Wardell, the 100- and 220-yard runner-up, they still didn't have a time equal to ours. The odds-on favorite for the 880-yard relay was the team from Laurel Highlands.

I felt confident but concerned about our chances and said, "The only way we can lose this race is to drop the baton!"

When the final call for the 880-yard relay was announced, we stood at the starting line together as the starter gave us our instructions. I looked at the stands and saw Mr. Kachur give me the thumbs up sign and smile. This was the moment he'd been waiting for.

Chase was our lead man, Bobby was second, I was third, and Bill came last. We'd done it so many times before, but this was the race that counted. The starter told the second and fourth runners to go to the other side of the track to their assigned exchange zones. While the first runners were preparing their starting blocks, I took my position in the third exchange zone.

"Runners, stand at your blocks!" The starter checked to make sure all was clear at the second exchange.

"Runners, take your mark!" The crowd held its breath. "Get set..." *Bang!* Chase took off around the bend. He seemed to have made up the stagger and opened a five-yard lead. Bobby anxiously awaited the exchange. As Chase neared, Bobby began his start.

It looked like a smooth pass. Then suddenly I saw Bobby run back. He had dropped the baton!

The oncoming runners quickly overtook him, and we went from first place to last in a heartbeat. I happened to glance at the stands and saw Mr. Kachur give a gasp of disbelief before he slumped over his knees. I wondered if he was having a heart attack.

Bobby retrieved the fallen baton from the grass and began his leg of the relay in last place. When I received the baton from him, my only thought was to catch as many people as I could to give Billy a chance. I probably ran the fastest 220-yard dash of my life. No one got any time splits, but I know I was under twenty-two seconds and moved us up to third place, but that wasn't enough. Stroders and Wardell were anchoring their respective teams.

With a five-yard lead, it would take a miracle to overcome that distance. Billy finished third. Everyone was disappointed by that turn of events. We met Mr. Kachur in stunned silence. He knew we were upset. Although he was disillusioned and disheartened, he tried to put things in perspective by saying, "Who would've thought that you'd drop the baton today?" He was right. In the entire season, we'd never dropped the baton once.

The lesson I learned that day was to never ignore the little things in life. You often get only one chance, and you must be at your best to take advantage of an opportunity. If not, you face a lifetime of regrets, saying, "If only I'd…"

A CHANGE OF PLANS

After graduation I had to decide what I truly wanted to do. Personally, I still wanted to join the Air Force. Going into the military always seemed like a great option. My parents, especially my Dad, still insisted I go to college. Money was still so tight. My parent's financial woes always seem to be mounting. In my way of thinking, the military was my only and best option. I could enlist and save money for college.

My guidance counselor, Mr. Thomas Crofcheck, did some inquiring on my behalf. He discovered that California State College in California, PA was beginning a new program attempting to bring in minority students. The program was to begin in the summer of 1969. It would last 16 weeks. Upon successful completion, you would earn fall entrance into the college and gain 3 credits towards the work completed in the summer program. The program was being financed by the state so the cost was minimal.

I, along with my good friend Melvin Early, signed up for the program. We began our daily journey down to California with a school friend, Linda Russell. We called her Rusty! It was fortunate for us that Rusty had a car because neither Mel nor I had transportation to and from college.

We were enrolled in English, mathematics, earth science, reading & literature for the summer months at Cal. It was an enjoyable experience. There were a lot of very interesting people that were a part of this program.

The professors were very dedicated, fair, and very demanding teachers. The sole function of the pre-college program was to see if you had the ability it takes to continue your education at a collegiate level. Many of the participants fell by the way side due to lack of interest, poor work and study habits, or simply laziness.

College wasn't for everyone our science professor once alluded to in a lecture that he gave one day. In his speech he talked about the many other needs of society not just in the academic community but in the daily work force. I understood completely what he was talking about but some of my peers simply missed the point altogether.

During that summer, between classes, I had the

opportunity to play basketball at the college gym, Hamer Hall. It was at this point I began to meet many of the freshman ball players that had been recruited for the upcoming season. They knew nothing about my high school background only that I wasn't a recruit to the program.

A few of the individuals that I had run track against in high school, Wes and Charlie Ramsey, were in the basketball recruiting class. They had both been a huge part of the Frazier High School basketball success in 1968 and 1969 when they were runner-up in the State Class B Championship to Mansfield High School, led by 7-footer Tom McMullen.

Wes and Charlie were both outstanding athletes. They were extremely athletic and played an aggressive style of basketball that would intimidate any opponent—but not me. I loved that style of play. That's how I was raised and they knew it.

We would often team up and play some of the other freshmen recruits. Time and time again we would send them off the court with their tails between their legs because we dogged them out on the floor. There was some resentment but we didn't care. We played the game the way we had been taught. We played it hard and fast!

Playing against the freshmen recruits gave me a big boost of self-confidence that I could continue my basketball career at the collegiate level. At least I was willing to give it my best shot!

I continued my daily studies and my recreational play at Hamer Hall and on the playgrounds at home. I told Mr. Taylor about my playing with the freshmen recruits. He encouraged me to try and make the team as a walk-on in fall.

ACCEPTANCE INTO COLLEGE

I still wasn't 100% sure if I wanted to do it but my dad told me that I should try it for a year and if I didn't like it, I could withdraw and enlist in the Air Force. I figured one year is not so bad. So I agreed and in the summer of 1969 I was enrolled as a freshman at California State College.

This had special significance for the Ross household because now Mr. and Mrs. Theodore E. Ross had not one but two sons in college. This was a historical day for our family.

At California, I was a resident of McCloskey Hall. Melvin, my good childhood friend, resided in Johnson Hall which was just down the street. There were a lot of Laurel Highlands' graduates on campus. Rusty had qualified; Susan Babbony, the former LH cheerleading captain, was living at a girl's dormitory on campus. Another special friend, Reathea Otto; was a daily commuter to college, and also a Laurel Highlands Graduate.

I had a boyhood crush on Reathea when we were in high school but I, being very shy and a little backward, never truly pursued the matter. Reathea had a great personality. She was a person you could easily talk to and she always had a wonderful smile on her face. We just remained friends for life. Reathea's mom worked in the business office at Cal. I would occasionally see her and she would always remind me to behave myself and hit the books.

I tried to schedule most of my classes in the morning so that I could be free in the late afternoon to attend the open basketball training sessions. I wasn't known by the coaches because I hadn't been recruited so this was my proving ground.

I knew several of the freshman recruits because I had played with them during the summer session. There were many that I didn't know however. Many didn't like the fact that I was there because I was a threat to their position. I didn't mind. I was going to prove to the coaches and my peers that I deserved to be there and that I could play.

When official practice rolled around on October 15, my birthday, I was the only walk-on to make the team—everyone else was a recruit. That was a huge honor for me!

My freshman coach, Mr. Floyd Shuler, was a tremendous coach and a great motivator. He taught me so much about not only basketball but life. Coach Shuler didn't care where you came from or how many honors you'd won or the number of all-star teams you were a part of. All he cared about was your willingness to work hard and improve. He pushed me both academically and athletically. I can honestly say that during that year I had significant growth as a true student-athlete.

We had an awesome freshmen and men's team that year. Our freshman team posted a record of 18 -2 and the Men's team won the Pennsylvania State Conference Championship for the first time in the school's history, earning a trip to Kansas City for the national tournament. What an accomplishment!

I was extremely proud of our team accomplishments but I was even prouder of my academic success. I was getting to the point that I found academia fun and enjoyable. Maybe it was the forced study hall all the members of the freshmen team had to attend. Or the close kinships that were starting to develop between players. All I knew is it felt like I was home again with the guys. It felt good.

Adapting to the College Environment

Being a member of the basketball team didn't allow for much free time. We had to schedule our class in the morning and early afternoon. We needed to be done by 3:00 PM. We had to attend a study hall upstairs in Hamer Hall from 3:00PM–4:15PM and after study hall we were to go directly to the locker room to get taped and dressed for practice. Practice would begin at 4:30 PM and last until 6:30 PM. After practice we would run over to the dining hall and hope that there would be something left to eat if the doors were still open. On several occasions we would get to the dining hall so late that there would be absolutely nothing left to eat. So we would fill up on soda drinks, ice cream and cake.

Normally, I would get back to the dorm between 7:00PM and 8:00PM. I'd spend some time with the guys in the recreation room watching TV or play a little ping pong. Sometimes I would just go outside and take part in the dormitory softball game that took place in the field between McCloskey and Johnson Hall. Afterward, I would retire to my dorm room, recopy my notes from class and prep for tomorrow's routine.

In addition to the daily routine, members of the basketball team had an imposed curfew of 11:00PM on weekdays and 12:30AM on weekends. Coach Witchey would often come and check to see if the curfew was being violated. I never broke curfew, however, I can't say that about a few of my teammates.

I didn't mind the rigid rules established by our coaches; the mandatory study halls, curfew or not being allowed to join a fraternity. Most of the rules were established to give us, as incoming freshmen, the greatest chance of succeeding in college. I may have resented it a time or two but in the long run it was worth the sacrifice.

HOME FOR THE SUMMER

During the summer months I would go back home to Uniontown. I worked as a playground director in the projects. In the summer of 1970, the Laurel Highlands School District sponsored a playground. I was employed as one of the directors.

That was a great summer! The playground was open to all the kids, young and old, that lived at Lemon Wood. We had basketball, softball, table tennis, races, special event days, movies, cookouts and sleepovers. You name it we had it during that summer.

Even though I was playground director I also needed to continue to find time to practice and improve myself for the upcoming basketball season. So I was faced with a dilemma at times. I played for our neighborhood team called "The Acre Crew" in the Laurel Highlands Summer League. My cousin Gay Gay, LT, Cedric, Bruce, Tim Cherry, Junior Brown, June Bug, our "Blue Eyed Soul Brother" - Jeff Crawford and Porky Braxton made up the team. Our games were scheduled at the various playgrounds in the district.

For some reason, the playground supervisor, Mr. Paul Hartford, didn't want me to participate in the adult basketball league. I would generally work out a schedule with a co-worker to take an hour or so off to attend the league game and then come right back. On one occasion, Mr. Hartford saw me playing at another site and went back to Lemon Wood and closed the playground because he said that I needed to be there. He wanted to fire me at that point!

I knew that I needed the money so I assured him that I wouldn't do it again unless I took the evening off to play on my time. I talked to Mr. Taylor about my situation and he tried to work out a schedule they would have many of my games played at Lemon Wood Acres. This way I wouldn't have to leave the playground. Mr. Taylor understood how important it was for me to continue to play during the off season.

THE ACRE CREW

That summer "The Acre Crew" took on all comers. We didn't have a lot of size, Gay Gay being the tallest, but we made up for it with speed and quickness. Our aggressive man to man style was unrelenting. Also, playing at the Acre court was a huge home court advantage for us. The one rim was about 10'6" while the other was 9'10." It was a little hard to get used to in a game. In addition to the rim variations the court was very long and narrow. This was great for teams that like to run up and down and who played a swarming man to man, trapping style of play like the Crew.

Eventually we were not permitted to have any games at the Acres. It wasn't because of the court; it was because of the rowdy fans. The Lemon Wood fans would come out in huge numbers to support their local favorites. It's very intimidating to have individuals standing around the court, screaming and hollering at your every move. Often times play would be interrupted because a fan may be instigating a fight with an opposing player. This scenario happened once too often, so play was suspended at the Acres.

Never the less we still were just as intimidating on the road. We made it through the regular season undefeated. We had to play the Clark team in the best of three championships on their home court. They had some very good ball players. Ricky Trainor who was an eventual standout basketball player at Waynesburg College; Tim Lulich, high school basketball player and cross country and track star at IUP; my state championship teammate, Bill Martin; and several other outstanding players.

We make it an easy conquest by winning the first two games handily. The Clark court was made to order for the Acre Crew. It was big and wide. It was made to order for our style of play. We pressed full court from baseline to baseline. We were the East Coast version of the Runnin' Rebels of UNLV. After the game we walked home with a deep sense of satisfaction that we had won the first Laurel Highlands Basketball Summer League Championship.

SOPHOMORE YEAR AT CAL

Summer was a blur and before you knew it, it was back to Cal for my sophomore year. I had made many new friends on the basketball team. We were starting to become a family because of the success we had from the previous season. Only three players from the men's team had graduated, two of whom played significant roles in its previous success. With the addition of some key younger players from the sophomore ranks and the veterans, it looked on paper like Cal had a winning combination. Unfortunately, talent without leadership is destined to falter as was the case for the California State College Men's Basketball Team of 1970–71.

When I was growing up I never thought about segregation or racism in

Uniontown. I lived in the projects but never realized that the two rows of black tenants were set up to segregate us from the white tenants. We still all played, laughed and worked together daily. I never thought about why, when I was in grade school, we would pass several other elementary schools on our bus ride to Phillips Elementary. I didn't think of the reason why Blacks could not swim at certain pools and Whites could. Or why some parks and playgrounds were made up of mostly Blacks in the East End and Whites in other neighborhoods in the western sections of the city. I had never had any racial slurs spoken to me or any of my friends. I did see that some individuals had some hostile attitudes towards people of color but they seemed to be a minority. When I went to college I think for the first time in my life I started to experience these attitudes of racism and prejudice as I went through my college years.

During my sophomore year as a member of the men's basketball team I had my first true test of character. Many of the older players grew up much differently then I. We did not share the same outlooks on life. Many of them often felt that I saw the world through rose colored glasses. I don't know if it was true but I was brought up to believe that if you worked hard you could overcome every obstacle in your path. The obstacle that I now faced was adult peer pressure.

Many of the older players had begun to complain

about the head coach, Myles Witchey. Coach Witchey had been the men's coach for several years. He was very knowledgeable, a fanatic about weight training and often very personable. The only fault that I found with him is that he tried to please everyone and because of this the rules were not set in stone. That's why a sense of favoritism seemed to exist within the team during that period. Players felt and resented this deeply. Many of the Black players seemed to feel that it wasn't favoritism but racism that was the real issue here.

I didn't see it that way during that time so when the Black upper classmen on the team approached me about participating in a basketball boycott by the Black players I had to decline. I honestly felt that Coach Witchey and Coach Shuler had always been open and fair with me. The things that the veterans were saying I just didn't agree with. The veterans understood my position and accepted it. So Cleveland Steward and I were the only Black ball players that were not going to be a part of the boycott.

This stance put me at odds with many Black students on campus during the turbulent years of the early 70's. I was beginning to feel a little uncomfortable but I still had my basketball family to lean on during this time.

Uniontown was not far from the college. The basketball boycott was beginning to gain local and some national media press but what was also apparent was that it wasn't being supported by all the Black ball play-ers, me in particular. Cleveland had changed his mind so that left me as the only hold out. I was bound and determined to play. However, there were outside forces that attempted to change my mind.

A couple of days before the actual game between 11:00 PM and 12:00 AM, a group of football players num-bering 12 to 15 came to visit me in my dormitory room. They instructed my roommate, Rege Stephenson, who was White, to leave the room. Rege left and I was con-fronted with an ultimatum. The spokesperson told me in no uncertain terms that I better reconsider my stance about playing. I told him that I would not. He informed me that if I did play that I would never be safe on this campus for the rest of my college career. I still stood my ground and said that it was my decision and I had talked it over with the other players. I was going to play!

As they opened the door to the hallway and began to file pass me I noticed that there was quite a crowd in the hall. It was most of the members of the upper floor of McCloskey Hall, my fellow dorm mates. They had armed themselves with baseball bats just in case an altercation was to occur. Fortunately nothing happened that evening.

I don't know if it's a mother's intuition or a sixth sense but I don't know how my mother found out that something was going on but she did. The next thing I knew was she wanted me to come home. The next day, she talked to my Aunt Betty. She, in turn, called her son-in-law Jerry Washington to drive down to California with my brother, Ted, and my cousins Buzzy and Gary to bring me home.

When the convoy arrived at the dorm, I was ordered to get my stuff and come home immediately. Before I was to leave, Ray Greene, our team captain, wanted to talk to me. I told my cousin Jerry that I needed to talk to Ray before I left for home.

I went to the outside snack bar in front of Herron Hall and met with Ray. Jerry took up a position near the outside railing with my brother and my cousin posted nearby. I talked to Ray for several minutes. He wasn't attempting to talk me out of anything but to reassure me that it was my decision to make and he and the other boycotters understood. After all was said, Ray and I shook hands and walked in opposite directions. As I approached Jerry, he opened his jacket to show me what he had brought along for security. I was happy that he didn't have to show his might but felt assured that the family was ready to react if necessary.

That's one thing that I could always say about the Ford Family which I am proud to be a part of. We have this family saying that states, "If you mess with one of us, you mess with all of us." This was quite apparent on my day in question and I'm truly blessed to have such a support system.

At home Mom explained why she sent for me. I

explained to her my thoughts and feelings on the matter. My parents had always raised my brother and me to be independent thinkers. That was one of the reasons we were able to attend college and didn't get hung up with all the nonsense that had plagued many Black youths in our communities. I said, Mom, I'm going to play!" Mom didn't argue with me about it. She did say however that the family would be in attendance at the game, just in case.

On Saturday, I drove back to California to make the team bus to Pittsburgh. We would be playing Point Park College at the Pitt Field House that evening. The mood on the bus was a little somber. Many of the ball players were happy that they would be getting a chance to play. Some wanted to prove a point that we didn't need the other players; I just wanted the whole ordeal to be over as soon as possible.

Once we got to the Fieldhouse we mulled around for a while and then went to the locker room to get taped and dressed for the evening contest. I had dressed quickly and was sitting quietly as the other players began to muster up. Coach Witchey and Coach Shuler began their pre-game talk. They discussed what offensive we would start with, they went over Point Park's strengths and weaknesses and our defensive calls. We had our team prayer and then we started out to the floor. As I rose to get in line, Coach Witchey stopped me.

He said, "Danny, I can't let you go out their dressed."
I said, "Coach, I want to play!"

"I know you do but this isn't just about basketball, it's about your college future and life on campus."

With that, Coach asked me to get changed that evening and I could still support the team by sitting on the bench. That's what I did that night. I watched my teammates win a close victory over Point Park College. I saw my teammates in the stands watch and I wondered what they were thinking about. I still don't know what if anything was proved by the boycott. I don't think it helped to unify the team. I think it had a negative effect on the program for years to come.

When I think back about that period, I often wonder if I would have done anything differently. My answer is no! Not one thing. What I learned as the years went on was that in order to have a team, you have to treat your number fifteen player the same way as your number one player. The rules and standards should apply to everyone equally.

THE DREAM

Basketball and college were different for me after that time. Another thing that had a profound effect on me was my father's passing. Early in the season, we were to participate in the Quantico Virginia Basketball Classic. The tournament was to be held during the winter holiday break. Before the tournament I was home on break in Uniontown, enjoying the companionship of family and friends. Many of my close friends were home from college or military service. With them around, the holiday season was special once again. Unfortunately, that holiday would take on a dark memory that would follow me for the rest of my life.

On the day before I was to return to California to resume practice, I visited with Crew members. Mom washed a few things for me to take back with me that evening, and Dad watched the news while chatting about school.

That evening, when I retired for the night, I had trouble sleeping. Anxious to return to school and begin practice, I was excited about the upcoming trip to Virginia with the team.

As I tossed and turned, I dreamed my father was in great distress. He showed signs of having another heart attack and was in severe pain. The dream was so vivid, I got out of bed and went to my parents' bedroom to make sure Dad was all right. Seeing everything was okay, I returned to my room and tried to rest.

When I awoke the following morning, I was tired from a restless night. I began gathering my possessions to pack my bag, and I had to do a lot of running around, not to mention visiting friends before I left.

After I finished my early morning errands, I started serious packing. While I did, Dad was extremely jovial, telling jokes and fooling around. He rarely did that with me or my brother, but that day he felt good. It was great seeing him that way. He'd been through a lot of pain and suffering since his stroke. With his partial paralysis, he had difficulty walking, but his mind remained sharp.

Dad continued in his upbeat fashion until my friend and roommate, Jerry Slampak, knocked on the door, and I knew it was time to go. As I said good-bye to my parents, I didn't know that was the last time I'd see Dad alive.

Once we arrived on campus, we found the college deserted. Only members of the men's basketball team and a few wrestlers were there. We were being housed in Clyde Hall, a men's dorm, during our stay. Jerry and I moved into our assigned room as other players arrived. We fooled around briefly, talking about our holiday and wondering how the coach would torture us at practice. As a group, we walked to Harmer Hall for taping and a team meeting. Coaches Witchey and Shuler conducted a brief meeting and laid out the practice plan for the week. Afterward, we went to the gym to begin our three-hour practice.

An hour later Coach Witchey was called to his office for a telephone call. He came back and called me aside. "Dan, I'm sorry, but I have some bad news. Your father had a massive heart attack a short while ago, and he passed away." I was stunned. I wanted to run, but where? I didn't know, but the feeling persisted.

"Someone's coming from your home to pick you up," he added. I left practice and waited for my ride, my thoughts racing. If I'd been home, I might've saved his life, I thought, a feeling that haunted me for decades.

Looking back, I think Dad's last day on earth was meant to be as it happened. The LORD gave him strength to shed the pain and suffering for one last day, and he gave Dad that sense of heaven he'd soon receive when he entered into the Kingdom. That was what made him so happy. He wanted to share that last moment of fear not for peace is at hand with me.

MY FIRST LOVE

With all that happened to me during my college sophomore year, on and off the court, I began to keep to myself. I had my good dorm friends, my close high school friends and my basketball family. That was my world and there really wasn't time for much else until I met my first college girlfriend—Linda.

Linda and I met at my friend Susan's dorm. I don't think she liked me at first but I won her over as time went by. She was older than I, more sophisticated and she was also White. I never really thought about interracial dating. I had always thought about people as people but during that era it was quite the contrary.

Race became more and more prevalent in daily life and society. I saw separate White and Black fraternities and sororities on campus. I saw the different signs for Black Power and the various militant groups there that were evident on campus. Everyone seemed to be a part of some group and normally based on ethic or cultural origin. I too was a member of a group and that was Alpha Beta Basketball. That was our basketball fraternity because we weren't allowed to join a chapter so we created our own.

I spent time with my basketball family, my few close friends and Linda. All of my friends liked Linda. She was a wonderful person. I too loved her but I wasn't sure of what type of commitment I was ready for back then. I was a very young college student. I was also extremely immature for my age. I had never had a girlfriend in high school. Sure there were a few girls that liked me but I was never into the dating scene. Linda scared me in a sense because she was older and more aware of what she wanted to do with her life. She seemed to have it all together. I, on the other hand, was just beginning to experience my new sense of freedom and discovery.

Linda and I went together for several years. She was my first true love but I wasn't ready to receive love then. Nature has a funny way of testing you. I failed my test with my first love but I'm fortunate to have experienced love and saw the sacrifices that she made that I couldn't make. When she told her parents about us, they disowned her. One of her girlfriends refused to allow me to attend her wedding because I was Black which ended their friendship. Linda made many attempts to signal her true feelings for me but I was too stupid then. My true regret is that I wasn't ready at that time to make a life with someone else because I hadn't made a life for myself. I guess it is true that you have to have self love before you can have true love for someone else. It took me a long time to learn that lesson.

Basketball season saw the end of a Black player boycott, the death of my father, my first girlfriend and the start of my collegiate track and field career. Track and field was always a love of mine. If I had gone to Rider College, in addition to playing basketball, I would have participated on the track and field team. During my freshman year at California they did not have a track and field program. In the spring of 1971 California State College began its first collegiate track and field program which I was a member of.

Mr. Marty Uher was the men's track and field coach in 1971. He was an instructor in the physical education department with emphasis on human movement and development. Mr. Uher had a very scientific approach to coaching track and field. This was very different from my high school coach, Mr. Kachur, who was a little loosey-goosey style. Everything was scheduled down to the very last second what we were to do with Mr. Uher. A few of the runners were individuals that I had competed against in Fayette or Washington County over the years in high school. Now we were teammates trying to make history as a part of the 1st collegiate track and field team at California State College.

We would hold the first collegiate action at the new Adamson Football Stadium. Our first meet would be against Bethany College. At the meet I became the first person to win a race for the inaugural team. As I placed first in the 100 yd dash; second in the 200; second place in the long jump; third place in the high jump; ran a winning leg of the 440 yard and mile relay team. What a start to my track and field career.

I had a great day and afterward Linda and I walked the two miles back to college. Boy was I tired! The next day, my friend Gary wanted to play a little one on one at Hamer Hall. I agreed. I had just come off a tremendous track performance. I was on top of the world.

Gary and I played one on one and then it happened. I went up for a shot and came down and twisted my ankle. It swelled up like a balloon. All I could do was hope and pray that I didn't break it. The hardest part for me was yet to come. I had to tell Mr. Uher about my accident.

Monday morning, I limped into his office. I could see that he was upset. When I told him what I had done he said, "You and that dang basketball"!

I felt stupid for what I had done. I had let him down but this injury was to plague me for the rest of my sport days, not only in track and field but on the basketball court as well.

LIFE'S WORK

The college years passed by quickly, I enjoyed being a part of the men's basketball program along with the track and field team. It helped me to stay focused with the academics and to help me budget my time effectively.

During my senior year I had a wonderful student teaching experience at two of the local schools. I did so well that upon graduation my college supervising teacher highly recommended me to the superintendent of a prestigious school district in the suburbs of Pittsburgh North.

I received a call from the district in August of 1973 asking if I would agree to come in for a comprehensive interview. I agreed and met with the assistant superintendent, Mr. Frank Christy for approximately three hours.

One of the first things that he related to me was that the office executive secretary had informed him about me and added that I was "Black." That didn't seem to sway the assistant, he still wanted to talk to me. At that time there were no Black teachers in this predominately White school system.

Mr. Christy was very candid with me. One of the first things he told me was my college supervisor, Mrs. Holman, called me, "The Pied Piper of Children."

He said, "That a beautiful title. What did you do in your student teaching to warrant such praise?"

I then began to talk to him about my student teaching experience; what I had learned; what I felt my strengths and weaknesses were; and my general philosophy of education. It was quite an event filled day for me.

I was happy with the way the interview had gone. Later Mr. Christy took me on an extensive tour of the district and talked in great length about the perceptions that many had about the community as being made up of all wealthy families. He showed me the true economic diversity within the district.

At the conclusion of the interview he told me that if a position did become available and if I was interested please give his office a call by Monday of next week. This was on a Thursday. When I got home I talked to my mom about the district and told her that I felt it would be a wonderful opportunity for me.

Right then, I had made up my mind. I was going to call and tell them that I would accept an elementary teaching position if one became available.

I called on Friday and was hired the following Tuesday. I became the first Black teacher to be hired in this Pittsburgh suburban school district. My Mom was excited for me but also a little fearful. She knew about the hardships that I would encounter but I knew that she felt in her heart that I was ready.

I met the gauntlet of challenges that were presented to a young Black man living and working in a predominately White community. I did it by treating individuals with the care and dignity that I grow up believing in.

I had a wonderful tenure as an elementary / middle school teacher and coach in the district. I served for thirty-three rewarding years receiving numerous awards both academically and interscholastically during that time.

With all the successes that I've had over the years, there isn't a day that goes by that I don't think about my parents. The thought that often saddens me is that I never truly took the time to thank them for everything they did for my brother and me. They performed countless sacrifices to raise their sons. They had a dream for us to have a better life than them. That's why a college education was so important in their eyes. By the time I wised up, they were both gone but their goals had been realized.

The only thing I can do now is to pass on those life lessons I learned from them and encourage the kids of today not to make my mistakes. Every chance I get, I say, "It's easy in our daily lives to forget the important things. We need to take time to thank the individuals who have been special to us."

FINAL REFLECTION

An old African proverb says, "It takes a whole village to raise a child." Lemon Wood Acres in Uniontown, Pennsylvania, was my village. My family, neighbors, and the many friends I made during those years helped raise and inspire me. They're an intricate part of my heart and spirit. The many life lessons we all learned during our wonder years are more precious today than ever.

It's tragic that in this fast-paced world where we work and live we often ask kids to grow up faster than nature intended. We unknowingly deprive them of that special period in their lives that lets them laugh at their mistakes; view the world from an honest, childlike perspective; and, most importantly, learn what's truly important in life. These stories are dedicated to you!